Don't Push Me

Don't Push Me

Walking The Wheelchair Walk
with Spokes Ableman

The stories in this book reflect the author's recollection of events. Some names, locations, and identifying characteristics have been changed to protect the privacy of those depicted. Dialogue has been re-created from memory. Spokes Ableman's dialogue is satirical.

Ed Hooper and Spokes Ableman

ISBN: 1507843321
ISBN 13: 9781507843321
Library of Congress Control Number: 2015901913
CreateSpace Independent Publishing Platform
North Charleston, South Carolina

ACKNOWLEDGMENTS

First and foremost, this is for my wife Cindy and our wonderful family. Cindy's love is why I'm even here. Chapter Fourteen is itself an acknowledgment of the many friends who have helped me along the way. I love every single one of you. Thank you Jonathan Rafert for your talent and help in the cover design. And a very special thanks and love to Lucy Painter, Mary Johnson, and Besty Wilford who helped in the editing of *Don't Push Me*.

DEDICATION

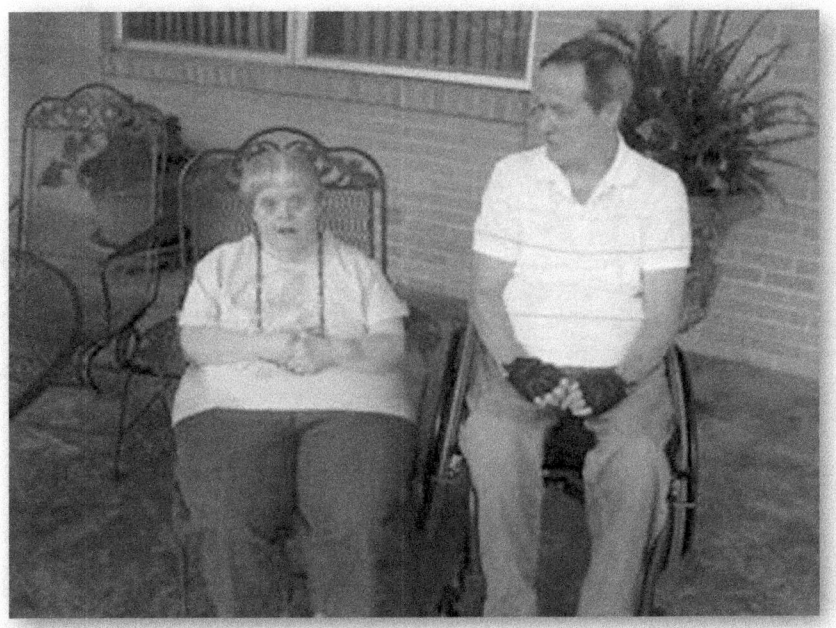

I dedicate *Don't Push Me* to my mother and my sister Cathy. Cathy had Down Syndrome and died during the writing of this book. My mother was Jean Cassidy Hooper Anderson. Her husband died when she was 29, and she raised four children on waitress wages as a single mom. She was rock-strong with a soft center, a hero who fought the demons of loss, and was able to save everyone, except herself.

TABLE OF CONTENTS

WHEN THE TRACKS ARE GONE

How do they remember to grow straight
    those oiled trees
    that blink by
while you and the cows,
dull to the changing sky,
wander the same rusty tracks?

                        Outside,
word is, they're being tore up
       the tracks lead to dirt;
word is, the rails forgot the way
       the same places have new names.

You've been parallel too long:
never able to travel left or right
eyes shaped through gaps in the boxcar
stealing past slitted landscapes.

Word is, that's all changed.
You're in the last boxcar
a wheelchaired hobo
                  squinting
at the wildflowers.

INTRODUCTION

I was rummaging through my old writings and I happened upon my rejected manuscript *Tin Cups, Tin Soldiers,* a compilation of articles I had written about the disability experience. A wonderful New York agent, Anita Diamant, really liked the script and tried unsuccessfully nine times to place it in large presses. The main criticism was that it was too difficult of a subject, i.e., disability rights and disability itself. Here is the end of her parting-of-the-ways letter in 1989:

> This may simply be ahead of its time for commercial presses. We would strongly urge you to continue sending this out – perhaps trying small presses. It's an excellent book. – Anita Diamant

I didn't send it to small presses. Most of the articles I used had already been published, and I was feeling pretty rejected so I boxed it up.

I opened the box again last week, and, lo and behold, the subject is as relevant today as it was 25 years ago, maybe more so. But it wasn't cohesive enough. It had no thread, nothing to hold it together. Plus, it was old, very old. It did have one thing, though. It had the introduction of Spokes Ableman, my alter ego. In almost every way, Spokes Ableman was the real birth of me totally accepting my disability. It's funny because there is a huge difference between becoming disabled and understanding what that means beyond the physical and mental trauma. In this age of Facebook, I often see posts by friends with disabilities that celebrate their re-birthday—the day they were injured or otherwise became disabled. Spokes Ableman, however, was always with me, but he became a transcendent catalyst—a character born when I realized that I was playing by a new set of rules. I didn't see that clearly until several years after my disabling injury.

Spokes could help carry the ball—or be the thread—I thought, and I started my rewrite. After all, I've had an extra 25 years of living with a disability to sharpen my focus and tell the story with more experience guiding me, and to add some humor by talking to my friend Spokes.

It is customary when introducing a book of nonfiction to tell what one's message is. But I feel compelled to start by saying what this book is not. It is not a woebegone dose of "pain and suffering" found in so many works about disability. It is not the "embittered cripple" depicted in uncountable numbers of both fiction and nonfiction, from Captain Ahab to Doctor No.

This book is not about overcoming anything, nor is it about courage in any shape or form. It is not Tiny Tim saying God bless the world either. There is enough printed and filmed material about all these ignorant, stereotypical portrayals to fill an entire wing of the library—all under the loathsome heading "The Handicapped."

As Spokes would say, "Piss on pity!"

Don't Push Me is about dramatic change, discovery, standing up for one's self, and living a happy life with what I call "this onerous yet precious gift called disability." It's about walking the wheelchair walk. I use Spokes Ableman to both lighten the load and to get to the very heart of it. It's about how my disability affected me, a so-called *normal* person before my injury in an automobile accident. And, more importantly, how and why I reacted with anger, amazement, ambition, bemusement, and even humor at both the subtle and overt stigma society foisted on me.

I also want to explain, as best I can, how this dramatic change affected my wife, my family, and my friends. I thought for a long time that it was just about me. Me, me, me. But it has always been about everyone who ever loved me. I've said this many, many times: I would not be alive today without the iron-love of my wife Cindy.

A friend told me many years after the accident that the feeling in my old office was like I had died. They were in mourning. Wow!

The moment a person becomes disabled, doors start closing. In many ways, it's worse now than it was 25 years ago. I think the primary reason we get closed off from the "real world" is that society doesn't see us as "fitting in." We are, by our very physical appearance, different.

You became a member of the club that nobody wants to join, Hooper. You're a gimp; live with it.

That's Spokes again. You'll meet him in a few minutes.

Anyway, through some fear/hate/intolerance of imperfection we become society's most undeserved outcasts. *Don't Push Me* explores that "club" Spokes mentioned, the one everyone is so afraid of. As one who uses a wheelchair, I resent the stereotypes. I resent accepting back entrances and insipid stares in lieu of dignified ramp entrances and dignified living. I accept none of the images and roles society has heaped upon me. If this sounds bitter, it is!—*not* at my physical condition, however, but rather at how I am treated and perceived because of it. The message our society gives its disabled population or others they see as unfit is: "It's a personal problem. Adjust." Or, the befuddling telethon mentality: "Here's a buck and a tear; see ya next year." Or, the clincher: "Do everyone a favor, and end it all."

Surely there is a distinction as to what is a personal problem and what has been wrought by the world around us. If, for example, a non-disabled man encountered a locked restroom in an office building and peed his pants, would he blame his bladder or the locked door? Take a guess. Yet, if a wheelchair user found a stall too small to get him and his wheelchair inside—effectively locked out—and peed his pants, he would be perceived as having a personal problem.

So a simple rule can be applied for accessibility to our manmade world: When reasonable means are available, things should be made accessible for people with disabilities. Accessibility and non-discrimination are basically what the 1990 Americans With Disabilities Act (ADA) is all about. When the barriers are removed, so are the perceptions as to what is a personal problem and what is a societal problem. But, of course, getting from place to place is merely the tip of a gigantic iceberg.

The real barriers are attitudinal. How do people see us? Spokes would say they really don't see us at all. So how, indeed, with the historical and cultural deck stacked against us can mainstream society possibly see us as part of their world?

And with the media bombarding the public with "crippled economies," "crippled farmlands," "crippled administrations," and "crippled cripples," where can it possibly lead? For us, it leads nowhere. It leads to the same stereotypes we've been fighting since we learned we were disabled. So "the blind" will continually be "leading the blind," and our message of wanting to be treated as individuals will forever "fall on deaf ears." (By the way, aren't these ad nauseam phases *ever* branded as clichés and discarded?) Sometimes, after I have read or watched my umpteenth story about courage and the two P's: pain and pathos, I temporarily break down and want to scream, "*My God! How can I possibly stop this*?" And the answer jumps right back at me: I can't, not sitting back and taking it, I can't.

Spokes is a little more direct.

Hooper, you're not spitting into the wind; you're spitting into Hurricane Katrina.

Spoke's pessimism is justified. These unrelenting negative portrayals are what foster prejudice as our number one enemy. Uninformed judgments and opinions about disability are made so routinely that those who make them really believe that their ideas are founded in deep wisdom. These barriers are so big that they make the Great Wall of China look like a speed bump.

You know what else, Hooper? We are ten steps behind LGBT and Immigration when it comes to being seen as being included. The Gay and Lesbian and ethnic communities passed us in public opinion like we were standing still—or is that sitting still?

It sure seems that way. Then there are the pseudo-scientific folks who believe that they can obtain insights into disability by becoming "disabled for a day," using a wheelchair, earplugs, or a blindfold. It would only be slightly more ridiculous for a man to claim insights into menstruation by donning a dress and wearing a maxi-pad for a day. One cannot live another's life as if he/she were trying out a new pair of shoes.

How about a Tampon, Hooper, and a pair of cute pumps?

Shut up, Spokes.

Sorry, Mr. Sensitive.

Ironically, though, I believe it is our own prejudice—people with disabilities'—that hurts us the most. I think that the social prejudice against the mainstream acceptance of people with disabilities is so strong that, incredibly, even the person who is being cast out "understands" why. This is because we believe what we learn. We learn, perhaps more than anything else, to acquiesce under the pressure of being disabled, i.e., unable to do certain things; feeling unwanted; in the way; and suddenly we start getting treated like second-class persons. Perhaps most damaging, we feel like we have no control over our own lives. It is therefore difficult to feel good about ourselves, and with our self-esteem on the skids, we start believing the very things that oppress us.

Astonishingly, that self-image, I believe, is the same or worse now than it was in 1989. The reason for this decline is the dismantling of adequate rehab and peer support over the past 20 years. The vicious combination of skyrocketing medical costs, managed care, and the slashing of benefits has reduced much of our rehab to an expensive Band-Aid. All the things that really helped people cope are evaporating: Peer support, recreational therapy, and adjustment time. An uninsured spinal cord injured person is often in and out of rehab in three weeks. I've had colds that have lasted longer than that. How can someone adjust both physically and mentally from a catastrophic injury or disease in *three freaking weeks*? I had four-plus months! Yes, that is probably too long for today's standards because hospital stays have dramatically decreased over the years, but this particular problem extends far past efficiencies in treatment. There has been a reduction in both coverage and care that has inflicted great cruelty and devastating long-term consequences to people who have suffered catastrophic injuries (Chapter Twelve).

When legislators' eyes glaze over and they cut and cut and slash programs and funding for rehab that actually help those who desperately need it to rejoin society, there is an ugly underbelly of thinking that surfaces in the backs of some decision-makers' heads: "They probably had it coming anyway."

What we really need to learn is how to purge ourselves of the prejudices, taught by thousands of years of culture and society, so we can see our disabled selves clearly, not through society's distorted lens. Our full humanity is intact, despite the "fate worse than death" and preconceived mentality working inexorably against us.

To be fair, Hoop, there are five or ten able-bodied people in the good old U S of A who do get it.

Therefore, the book *Don't Push Me* is an eclectic look at my experience with disability. I wanted to do more than rationalize my situation. I am happy, a happy quadriplegic for almost 36 years now! And damnit, there must be a good reason for it. Most certainly my wife Cindy (especially, especially Cindy whom I often call Bunny) and my family and friends have a lot to do with my happiness.

I am not unique in that respect, however. I know many people with disabilities who feel like I do, who walk the wheelchair walk. Married, single, whatever. When you're disabled, though, being happy doesn't seem to be enough for the millions of knee-jerk observers. Smiles mean bravery to them. You inspire them by your mere presence. Why?

Or on the other side of the image, anger means bitterness. There seems to be no middle ground. So, I sat down with my buddy Spokes to discuss the road traveled, to explain how my thinking about being disabled developed, and to show what really puts a smile on my face and what pisses me off.

All the works included were written after I realized that I was disabled, most written now, a few written then and updated. I was paralyzed, yes. But I like to make a distinction between having a disability and knowing you are disabled. That "click" of realization that I was suddenly playing life's game under a different set of rules than so-called normal people didn't really hit me until I went back to college (Chapter Six). That, for me, was the beginning of knowing I was disabled, and knowing that many of my problems were caused by outside forces beyond my control, and, before then, beyond my comprehension.

Shortly after my college fiasco, a vocational counselor gave me a beat-up looking subscription ad for the *Disability Rag*, published out of Louisville, Kentucky. I figured, what the heck? So I sent in five dollars (that's right, five!) and asked if the magazine accepted poetry. Mary Johnson, the *Rag's* editor, replied that the *Rag* used few poems, but to send her something, anyway. I did. I sent my poem "The Way Downtown," and much to my delight it was published. Right after "The Way Downtown" was published, I received a letter from one Joseph L. Baird, Senior Professor of Medieval Studies in the English Department of Kent State University. He wanted to use my poem in a book of poetry that he and Deborah Workman were editing about the disability experience. I have two poems in Baird's and Workman's *Toward Solomon's Mountain: The Experience of Disability in Poetry* published by Temple University Press.

Mary encouraged me to write about my experiences, showing the personal and social tangle involved in living with a disability. I chose to open the book with my short poem "When The Tracks Are Gone," because it best describes my feelings about the confines of prejudice, and the need to survive the changes and negative emotions, lest I let my life's tracks be shortened to where I forget how to—or don't want to—live in the mainstream world.

I offer *Don't Push Me* to be of use, for society to hear a fresh voice. If I can expose, laugh at, and explore the experience of living with a disability, then I will have in some measure succeeded by having people understand that my life—every life, disabled or not—needs to be afforded dignity, equality and respect. None of us should be coerced into settling for less.

A Few Words About Usage (see Chapter Thirteen):

Since people with disabilities don't have commonality innate in their very being, like Blacks have their skin color and woman have their gender, trying to come up with a name that pleases everyone seems impossible. I will occasionally use "disabled person" (although imprecise) to describe a "person with a disability" because the wordiness of "person with a disability"— however accurate—can be incompatible with style. And at least we get "disabled" and "person" in the same phrase. None of my usage is meant, in any way, to infer or imply the individual him/herself is either unable or something less of a person. As for Spokes, he is liable to say anything.

PREFACE

The Origin of Spokes Ableman

I met Spokes Ableman in 1980-something, and he was and is me. No, I'm not schizophrenic. Spokes is my self-realized self, my disabled self. I'd always been a big fan of Chicago Tribune writer Mike Royko who would periodically write a column using a cabby. Royko would talk to him, an everyday taxi driver with everyday views on the world. Obviously, the cabby was Royko himself but the conversations ranged everywhere from hilarious to poignant.

I had written a story about an imaginary person with a disability. I named him Spokes Ableman. He was a paraplegic, or in the vernacular a "para." Here is that story:

Spokes Ableman, my new, aggressive, outspoken friend, and I were sitting outside Sears talking. He was telling me about another time he'd been sitting in the shopping mall:

I was people-watching—mostly women—when this 4 or 5-year-old kid and his mother came walking past.

"Why is that man in that chair, Mommy?" The kid yelled out.

"Shhhhh, honey... It 's because he can't walk," his mother told him.

"Why!" The kid yelped, his voice echoing through the mall.

"Come over here, kid," I said to him. "What's your name?"

"Bobby, Bobby Wilkins," he told me. "What's your name, mister?"

"Spokes Ableman. But you can call me Spokes, Bobby."

"Leave the nice man alone, Bobby," the kid's mom said, then turning to me, "I'm sorry, Mr. Ableman."

"Don't worry about it, Mrs. Wilkins. Do you mind if I talk with Bobby for a minute?"

"Well, we really must be going," she insisted.

"Ah, come on Ma, jest for a little while. Pleeese!" Bobby pleaded

"Okay. Just for a minute." She cautiously gave in.

"Bobby, do you know what this chair is called?"

"No, Spokes, what?"

"It's called a wheelchair. And just like your mom said, I use it 'cause I can't walk. I use it to get around," I told him.

"How come?" He was a curious little guy.

"My legs don't work like most people's."

Then I thought I'd show him something.

"Hey, you wanna take a ride, Bobby?"

"Can I drive it, Spokes?" He asked me.

"No, kid, you can't drive it. But I can give a you a ride down to the coffee shop and buy you a Coke."

"I don't think so, Mr. Ableman," his mom told me with worry lingering in her voice.

"Call me Spokes," I told her again. "You can come too, have a coffee with us. What's your first name, Mrs. Wilkins?"

"Carolyn," she told me.

That all happened fifteen years ago, Hooper. It seems like yesterday.

I gave Bobby a ride down to the coffee shop—him smiling ear-to-ear, reaching for the push rims and trying to get at the brakes.

I found out Carolyn's husband was in Vietnam, too. He didn't make it home alive, though. After we talked for a good long while, I asked her if she'd go with me to a movie on Friday, and, to my shock, she said yes. Did I mention she was gorgeous?

A year later, we were married. Now we've got David, 13, and Sara, 10.

Bobby, I mean, Robert—he likes that better—is starting his third year of college this fall. He's a great kid.

Spokes stopped. Then after a few seconds, "Jesus, he's a great kid!" Spokes repeated, slapping his hand against the side of his chair.

This little slice of life story was the birth of Spokes Ableman, and a way to vent the birth of me totally accepting my disability. Spokes was never the same character after this story. But he turned into my outspoken alter ego (some would say not so alter). He became my smart-assed friend, who, in the mold of *Seinfeld's* Kramer tends to pop in and pop off at the damndest times. Sometimes he says a lot, sometimes not. He will often tell the truth and say what many of us think but don't dare say.

CHAPTER 1

CURE ME, CURE YOU

I couldn't help studying how briskly my wife was walking down the beach, cooling waves splashing up around her feet. Her footprints were like the cycle of life itself: making a firm impression only to be washed away, time and time again. How fleeting each wave, each footprint, each life is, I thought. We are here for a short time and then poof, gone. What footprint will we leave? Everyone with any sense of responsibility and belonging wonders that, don't they? It wasn't long until Cindy had walked out of sight. When I could no longer see her, it triggered an unsettling feeling of absence. I belonged at her side. I worried that the sea or fate might not let her come back to me.

Since my ability to make footprints in the sand was washed away many years before, I watched from my wheelchair on a wooden deck built out onto the beach area. I thought how magical it would be if Bunny and I could make that walk together like we once did, watching the gulls fighting over a scrap of food, and looking for shells, and kicking water back and forth at one another. If only I could, I thought. But then I saw she was on her way back, and the thought disappeared as quickly as the last wave that had splashed up on shore.

Not long after the beach experience, Cindy and I went to a restaurant inside a hotel. We passed a meeting room where a sign just outside read: "Faith Healing, Tonight." There must have been one hundred or more folding chairs lined up in there. I don't believe God will cure someone merely for attending these functions so I continued on to dinner, although I was curious as to what they do in these healing rituals. But the sign raised an intriguing question for me: If I could be completely cured, would I take the pill, the operation, the regeneration, the faith-healing. Would I take "The Cure" for my disability?

The question of cure was a stark departure from my on-the-beach thinking, from that childlike craving to walk to questioning whether I wanted to be cured at all. So, I pose the question to all of us with non-life-threatening disabilities: Would you take "The Cure"? I don't consider the question crazy, or easy to answer. I think, however, that most people would insist I belonged in a rubber room for even posing such a question. Everyone with a disability must want to be cured and live a "normal" life, society thinks. The astounding throngs that visit Lourdes each day, the millions of people (and dollars) taken in by the-hand-on-your-head healers, the deluge of tears spent on telethons, the "cure" projects collecting both dollars and accumulating that infinite human currency: hope. These are ample proof for most people as to the agony of disability. People simply cannot imagine us—much less themselves —living a "good life" from the seat of a wheelchair.

That prejudice is what needs to be cured, *not me*! And that prejudice runs deep. Certainly it is what we have learned, but it also had to have begun far back in our evolution, wired in like survival itself. Cavemen who broke a leg probably didn't last too long in the tribe. And the animal world still ostracizes its members all the time. In the wild, it *is* survival of the fittest and the weak, broken or different ones are banished or lag behind and are killed. It still breaks my heart when I see on Animal Planet how the meerkats cast out a member of their group, and how that one lonely meerkat sits atop a hill looking anxiously here-and-there, doomed without the clan.

Humans are now civilized, mostly. We save and care for (well, that's debatable) our injured to be part of the tribe so-to-speak. But we with disabilities are not really accepted because the human tribe cannot truly digest this level of differentness. Prejudice has been used on every group imaginable: Blacks, Hispanics, Jews, Muslims, Women, Irish, Italian, Poles, Asians, Native Americans, Gays, the list is a long as history and no doubt longer. But people with disabilities are at the bottom when it comes to lack of acceptance. It's not hatred, however; it's fear and pity that secure us to the bottom like an anchor.

The heart of this book is about pushing back from the seat of a wheelchair and saying: I am not the problem; you are! Interestingly, women seem to empathize with the message far better than men do. Surprise, surprise.

We who have forged happy lives with our disabilities need to explore the nature of our happiness. I think my disability sat me down and had a long talk with me and kept talking all these years even when I wasn't fully listening. I'm happier now than I was before I broke my neck. I love my wife and my family more. I have a better rapport with most everyone. I wasn't a jerk (shut up, Spokes!) when I was still walking, but I am a better person now than I was before my disability. Hopefully, *Don't Push Me* is testament to that lesson and quality of life. Unlike those who presume to judge me, though, I don't have a compelling need to formulate my life's quality and compare it to any other person's to feel better. Still, if nothing else, this experience we have come to call disability has caused me to look hard at myself—at the nature of my existence. It begs the question; would I be a happier, better human being if I were cured?

After one lives with a disability for a period of time, it assimilates into his/her life experience. Walking—or seeing, or hearing—are experiences most of us who are disabled either can't remember or never had to begin with. The act of walking, for example, becomes as abstract a concept to wheelchair-users as getting around in a wheelchair probably is to walking people. We simply forget what it's like to walk, and it becomes relatively unimportant to us.

Whoa, whoa, whoa, Walking Eddie. Stop right there. What's walking got to do with it?

That's society's yardstick, Spokes. I don't need to walk again to live a happy life.

Again, Hooper, what's walking got to do with any of this? This is about having some of those normal physical functions, you know, the old BB & S.

BB & S?

Bowel, Bladder and Sex. Give me the BB & S and I'll roll through this world like a man who just won the lotto.

Like you don't have sex, Ableman?

Yeah, I have sex, great sex, but wouldn't you like to have your thrusters activated again? Or how about just taking a long, long leak? Whoa, baby."

Ok, Ok! But those are not the driving forces that control my life. I can't and won't obsess over something that I've learned to live with or without. Plus, skip ahead and read the chapter on sexuality, Ableman.

Oh, so I'm going to get sex-ed from you, blue-pill Eddie?

Whatever, Spokes.

Think of the upside for Cindy.

And what might that be, Ableman?

No worries about you peeing all over the toilet seat, or leaving the seat up and her falling in.

How is this relevant, Spokes?

It's not. Back to the point, Hooper, if someone offered you a magic pill, and, boom, you're cured. No pain. You'd take it?

No pain, and if it made my life easier, sure I'd take it. But there's no magic out there, Spokes.

So, you'll let others obsess over cure and if they're successful, you'll jump (excuse the expression) on the proverbial band-wagon. Is that it?"

No, I'm worried about that large group of people who spend virtually every waking hour waiting for the "cure news" while the years and their lives tick away until they grow old and become more lost and far more broken than their disability ever made them. Wallowing is empty, and the only footprint it makes is misery for the person and their loved ones. But it's amazing how one word keeps it going, "soon." It's coming "soon."

Come on, Hoop, you know that when the breakthrough comes, all of that goes away.

What's this role reversal? Now you're drinking the cure-tea, Ableman? I've been hearing and reading the breakthrough reports for 36 years. It hasn't happened. If something like stem-cell works for spinal-cord-injuries or even that new microchip technology or electrical stimulation,[1] that will be great for the future. As the saying goes, I'm getting too old for this.

True, some put life on hold, hoping a spinal-cord-injured lab mouse's legs will twitch and it'll start running around in circles. Whose job is it, I wonder, to break their little necks?

That's sick, Spokes. But we've been sitting for a long time.

Yikes! My legs and ass aren't going to win any beauty contests, that's for sure. So what happens if they infuse a jolt of feeling into those atrophied ducklings? Ouch!

Big ouch. You know the whole prospect of fixing the central nervous system is frightening. It's like trying re-do, re-attach, re-grow, bypass (whatever!) a tiny ball of fine, mushy, cut-up fishing line. And once the mice are running, who'll be the first human to be experimented on?

Hmmm, will there be short-circuits or dying batteries that cause some kind of herky-jerky, Mr. Roboto motion? Christ, china shop owners will be rushing to slap "Closed" signs on their doors when they see The Walking Cured approaching.

We become who we are because of our disabilities. You wouldn't be nearly the pain in the ass you are as an able bodied person, Ableman.

---

1 http://www.usatoday.com/story/news/nation/2 14/04/08/paraplegics-stimulation-paralysis/7420027/

Thanks, I think. Oh, oh, there's that look on your face again, Hooper. You're going to use the P-word aren't you?

You mean pride, Spokes?

You know exactly what I mean. Yes, pride. You always manage to sneak that into the discussion, like pride gives you a right to get on your soapbox and beam like the winner of some 8th grade spelling bee.

And what, Spokes, you're not proud of the life you forged with your disability?

Damn right. But humility and a cure are preventing me from taking my much-deserved bows.

Disability pride is important, very important. It helps us see ourselves in a light that we created, rather than the jaded light-show put on by society's special-effects department. Disability pride is difficult to explain. Accepting one's disability is part of it. The following stanza from "Testaments V," by James Weigel Jr., captures that acceptance for him:

> I would slip
> this glove of body off –
> humped, bony, sweated, sore –
> except the weary thing
> shows where I live.

Other people with disabilities are not the least bit weary in their own skin; they are empowered by it. Disabled people are beginning to say, "Here I am disability and all. Take me with it, or walk on by!" That's pride!

Many of us have earned our self-esteem, yet each of us knows humiliation, degradation, pain, pity, paternalism, prejudice, self-oppression, and discrimination; we've lived through them all. And survived! Have we survived only to strive for something that is now unnatural for us? Can we have disability pride and be cured as well? Would it not be impossible to have pride in something no longer a part of who we are?

Or, am I merely rationalizing my situation: making the best of a bad bargain? Is it stretching pride a bit too far to say that our essence as human beings would change because we are suddenly cured? Have we not learned enough from the disability experience to cope in the world as nondisabled people? Indeed, one is tempted to argue, if you can stay alive and psychologically upright in this world with a disability, surviving should be a snap without one. Right?

Finally, wouldn't the self-proclaimed improvements throughout my life have occurred, wheelchair or not? I wonder....

I'd guess that most people with disabilities have thought about "cure." For me, it started right after the acute stages of my injury when not an hour passed without me trying—hoping for some kind of divine intervention—to move my legs, my fingers, my toes. Hell, there are times even today when I'm tired and going to bed, and instead of just being able to flop in the bed and konk out, I'm struggling to pull my pants down, and I suddenly think, "Haven't I paid my dues? Does this have to be so much freaking work?" I don't try moving what won't move anymore. Still, once in a while my frustration surfaces, or nostalgia might take hold of me like it did at the beach, but only on rare occasions. And the effect goes as quickly as it comes.

My pensive thoughts are rare because I am not obsessed with "cure." There are, however, those who are tearfully or hopefully obsessed with it. What is only a fleeting thought for me can be either a continual wallowing in the past, or, an "if-only-I-were-cured" hoping. They see no pride in their existence, only misery, dependency and humiliation. Every able-bodied person who sees such suffering gets an instant recharge of negativity. But why should people with disabilities have to accept what they see as the cause of their misery: disability itself? It *is not* easy living with a disability, but it doesn't have to be needlessly intolerable for people, either.

There are really only two aggressive ways—suicide notwithstanding, yet too often chosen—to react to the circumstance and stigma heaped upon us: Either to fight for dignity with the disability or fight to be cured, which could peel off the stigmatic skin. We who subscribe to the former believe that people need to be cared for, and cared for now. It's urgent. Many people with disabilities need such help, by way of personal care, peer interaction and societal understanding. With our baby-boomers aging, we know how critical personal care is for quality of life. Home care is a booming business for seniors, but not so much for disabled folks. With proper care and/or independence, people with disabilities too can come to understand that they are still full human beings, and that they can live out each day with life's opportunities in front of them. However, if we cannot get our basic human needs taken care of, misery comes on like a tsunami and drowns any hope for a good life. It is simply that dismal.

We don't have to put life on indefinite hold hoping to be cured. We don't have to drag through each day like the one before until death starts looking like a good option. Moreover, we cannot cure everyone, and we cannot cure our way out of social responsibility. Care is the answer.

Nazi Germany had an interesting solution to cure people with disabilities.[2] They killed them, up to 300,000 by some accounts. The T4 pro-

---

2 http://www.bbc.co.uk/ouch/fact/the_holocaust_and_disabled_people_faq_frequently_asked_questions.shtml

gram initiated by Hitler himself was set up to purify the Aryan race from those seen as unfit and inferior. Seems Adolph too thought disability was "a fate worse than death," but instead of pitying them, he decided to do all those inferior folks a favor by killing them. The mass murders, starvations, and lethal injections were called mercy killings of "useless eaters" by the Third Reich's propaganda machine. T4 turned out to be a trial run and training ground for the Final Solution to exterminate the Jews[3]. Not surprisingly, T4 is also an obscure footnote in history.

Hitler didn't start with purifying genocide, though. In 1933, the German government instituted the "Law for the Prevention of Progeny with Hereditary Diseases." This law called for the sterilization of all persons who had diseases considered hereditary: mental illness, learning disabilities, physical deformity, epilepsy, blindness, deafness, and severe alcoholism.

Our solution can only happen with caring for those who need care through focused unity. There is a unity in our "differentness;" but we need to see it. With the Muscular Dystrophy Association, Multiple Sclerosis Society, Spina Bifida Association, United Cerebral Palsy Association, the National Spinal Cord Injury Association, and many others stacked separately on top of one another all vying for money, the "every-disability-for-itself" attitude forms only a dilemma: Which group will we leave behind to be society's final defects? It's not competition as much as it is separation. Care needs a unified focus, not each trying to cure and care for their own. Plus, we seem bent on sending our boys off to get their limbs blown off and their brains scrambled in one war after another. We can't seem to cure that. And we cannot cure our way out of the social quagmire in which so many people have been stifled for so very long. We cannot, "cure" or not—knowing what we know—turn away from our brothers and sisters.

---

3 http://www.history.com/topics/world-war-ii/the-holocaust

You know, Spokes, there are tons of people like you who succeeded with a disability, not without one. As I've said many times, you wouldn't be near the smart ass you are as an able bodied person.

Well, again, I thank you for those cunningly veiled words of kindness, Hoop.

But, would Itzhak Perlman play violin better without polio?

Could Franklin D. Roosevelt have run our country better?

Would we understand black holes (now gray holes) better if Stephen Hawkings could sing and dance the Watusi?

And would Stevie Wonder write and perform the same with 20/20 eyeballs?

Who knows, Spokes?

And who cares since they've become who they are with their disabilities, not in spite of them.

Did you know FDR was literally propped up to hide his disability? "FDR's Splendid Deception" by Hugh Gallagher chronicles Roosevelt's elaborate efforts to hide the effects polio had on him.

I know, Hoop, and there was a big controversy buzzing around the FDR Washington Memorial. Some absolutely didn't want FDR shown in a wheelchair. After a pretty good tussle, the truth won out and there sits FDR in a wheelchair.

Bill Clinton dedicated the FDR memorial in 1997, and said that the wheelchair being shown "was a way to make sure that the American people know that this great, great president was great with his disability."

Amen.

It might be interesting to know if these kinds of achievers would each turn in his/her disability—that thread intertwined into what makes their human fabric whole—to be "normal."

So, I asked several ordinary, happy, well-adjusted people who had been disabled for over 20 years if they would "take the cure." Each answer was the same: "NO!" One person took the realistic stance: too much uncertainty and pain. The other two, while weighing the obvious pain and risks, simply said "no" because they were happy the way they were. I don't believe that these people represent the majority; but they do represent a new idea, and none of them is stupid or mentally unbalanced.

Then I ran across this little bit of wisdom imparted by Ram Dass who had a near fatal stroke in 1997 and was paralyzed. Here are some excerpts from "Still Here":

Although my outward life has been radically altered, I don't see myself as a stroke victim.

Getting old isn't easy for a lot of us. Neither is living; neither is dying. We struggle against the inevitable, and we suffer because of it. We have to find another way to look at the whole process of being born, growing old, changing, and dying, some kind of perspective that might allow us to deal with what we perceive as big obstacles without having to be dragged through the drama. It really helps to understand that we have something—that we are something—which is unchangeable, beautiful, completely aware, and continues no matter what.

Recently, a friend said to me, "You're more human since the stroke than you were before." This touched me profoundly. What a gift the stroke has given me, to finally learn that I don't have to renounce my humanity in order to be spiritual – that I can be both witness and participant, both eternal spirit and aging body. The stroke has given me a new perspective to share about aging, a perspective that says, "Don't be a wise elder; be an incarnation of wisdom." That changes the whole nature of the game. That's not just a new role; it's a new state of being. At nearly seventy, surrounded by people who care for and love me, I'm still learning to be here now.

Dass really hit home with me here with "unchangeable, beautiful...continues no matter what," and "...not just a new role; it's a new state of being." It seems people with disabilities and older people have much in common, except disabled people don't want to face that they'll get old and old people don't want to admit they'll become disabled. Dass merges the two beautifully, and I think he would understand my life with a disability quite well; it's a new state of being.

I have toiled with what seems to be a simple problem, easily solved: Take any chance to leap out of my wheelchair and run like hell. If it were all that easy, I'd do it. But in exploring the how's and why's of "cure," I've discovered it's anything but simple.

I've returned to the beach. It's only fitting that I finish this chapter where I started it. I sit here and remember going to the shopping mall one day with my grandson, Jim. He was about 9 or 10 years old:

"Hey, Pop, can I ask you a question?"

"Sure, what?" I asked. I had no clue know what was coming next.

"How did you get injured, exactly?"

I told him the quick story: "I was driving home from a party and I fell asleep. The car hit a median strip bump and flipped end over end and my neck was broken."

He paused a while, and I was thinking that the next question was going to be: Did it hurt really bad? Was there lots of blood? Were you drinking? A dozen things, except what I actually got.

Jim then looked me square in the eyes and says, "If you think about it, Pop, if you weren't in that wreck, you wouldn't have spokesableman.com or the rugby team and all that other stuff you do. So in a way, it's kinda good, know what I mean?"

"I know what you mean," I responded, trying not to act shocked. "You know what else? If I wasn't in that accident, we would have never moved to Florida and your mom would have never met your dad, and you would have never been born." I thought that would totally blow his mind.

After a pause and an acknowledging smile, Jim said, "Good point, Pop. So, where's this t-shirt place?" And off we went.

I was pleasantly stunned. Jim got to the heart of it all. Life goes on with and without us. If you choose to go on, wondrous things can happen like the existence of two intelligent, talented, thoughtful, and loving human beings named James Edward and Alexander Charles who wouldn't be on this earth had I not been injured, or if I were cured. It's unlikely, but the choices we make might well change the history of our world. Most likely, though, my grandsons, like so many other children and grandchildren, will blend into the fabric of humanity. One thing I know for certain: They are already exquisite additions to this earth, and with all the hatred, violence, and polarization in our times, and even with all the cloudy uncertainty in front of us all, they make me feel optimistic about the future.

As the sun sets, I reflect on my wife, my children, my grandchildren, my family, my friends, those I love, my writing, my music, my disability, myself, and my life. What must they all think of me? Do even they really understand? I know about my mortality. I understand my limitations and imperfections. As the waves roll in, I see that all the fleeting footsteps on the shoreline have been smoothed away. I realize that it's not the physical impressions we make in life that endure, but the mental ones. I roll away knowing that I don't need to be cured. Somehow I survived. And I'm proud of who I've become.

Me too, Fast Eddie.

CHAPTER 2

THE CLUB NOBODY WANTS TO JOIN

Spokes, do you remember Chet?

You mean that retarded guy we fucked over when we were kids?

We didn't fuck over him, Spokes. He was a friend.

Oh, right, does the phrase "with friends like these..." mean anything to you, Hooper? Chet was that kid who, as rumor had it, was hanged by his brothers playing Cowboys and Indians in his backyard and had brain damage. He was like 4 or 5 when, supposedly, they strung him up.

Oh, come on, Spokes. We were young, just ordinary kids of 12 or 13; Chet was older, three or four years older. He was built like a sawed-off version of Steinbeck's Lenny. We thought he acted like it too, "funny," "touched in the head"—whatever.

Hooper, your own sister had Down Syndrome!

Yeah, but we were insulated from that and didn't really under-stand. Besides, Cathy wasn't like Chet. But do you remember what the previous generation of kids in our neighborhood did to Chet when he was 12 or 13? Remember that?

Of course I remember, Hooper. I was in the park that day, watching from a distance. How do you remember it?

That crew was especially mean. They often took Chet to the park and put him on the swings, and swung him high, far too high, and reveled in his squeals of both joy and fright. One day they decided to shove the swing high enough so that it would go up and around and over the top bar, you know, the way kids love to do with an empty swing, but they planned to do it with Chet in it. So they started pushing harder and harder, higher and higher, so that it created a kind of frenzy of pushing and squealing. Higher, higher and higher. Chet all the while squealing like a wild man. Slack began to get in the swing, and it began to give a bit and jerk up short with each push. Suddenly, in his terror, Chet jumped out and landed headfirst right smack on the slack wire fence opposite the swing. Then he really started screaming—wild, insane howls. Chet was bleeding and the boys were afraid of getting caught, so they crowded around their victim, mumbling, blubbering, comforting; trying desperately to stop the noise and the bleeding before someone came. For Chet, the pain and bleeding apparently subsided, and he began to mutter in that hoarse guttural voice of his, over and over again: "It's O.K., youse guys, it's O.K. I ain't hurt. It's O.K. It's O.K." Jesus! He was comforting them. And, yeah, he was ok after whatever pain he endured and the ten stitches over his right eye healed.

Oh, so when you new guys took over as Chet's "friends," you were vast improvements over that kind of shit, Hooper?

Yes, we were.

We all kind of liked old Chet, in our way. He thought the Three Stooges were the funniest of the funny. He sometimes watched the Stooges at our house and he would snort and laugh and slobber. He was actually funnier than the Stooges. On our duller days, we could hardly wait to see him coming, wobbling up the street on his rickety, old bicycle that looked a lot older than it actually was. He rode the damn thing all over town, and unless he got off to play with us in one of our games, that's about the only time we ever saw him, riding up and down the streets.

And what were some of those Mother Teresa games you played with 'ol Chet?

Well, Whip for one.

Oh, now that sounds really humane, Hoop. Do tell.

My kid brother Don, who was 6 years old at the time and therefore less agile than the rest of us, was always the Whip Man, wielding his "whip" made of a branch plucked off a bush that grew alongside our house. The object of the game was very simple: Don chased you till he caught you and then he'd whip the shit out of you. Sometimes, one of the older kids pretended to get caught, just to keep the game going. But the real object of the game was get Chet, who ran about as fast as I did on my hands and knees. Chet loved barreling around that house though. It seemed like he thought he was going a hundred miles an hour, laughing and carrying on, but he was hardly moving at all. Don would run here and there, helter-skelter, but would eventually hone in on Chet. When he caught 'ol Chet—as he always did—he would whip the living crap out of him. Chet would fall down with the first blow and just lie there, slobbering and laughing.

Oh, yeah, Hooper, you guys were far nicer to Chet than the swing guys.

Christ, Spokes, I don't know to this day whether he was doing it because he was having fun or because he had such a desperate need to be around us guys. We called him Chet the Jet.

Any other strokes of kindness, Hooper?

Well, yes.

One of the other games we called Park Benches or Bench Tag. We would get about eight or nine park benches and draw them up in a circle like covered wagons, making sure to leave gaps between each one and put one in the middle. Then we would play tag on the benches, never touching the ground. According to the normal rules of the game, if you hit the grass, you were it, but according to our rules, if you were Chet you were always it. So around and around those park benches we would go, with Chet lumbering behind. And, predictably, after a while Chet would go sprawling down between the benches—hard. And we would all go running over concerned-like, shouting, "Jet, Jet, are you all right?" And Chet would moan and groan, and saliva would be coming out of his mouth, and he'd mumble, "Oh yeah, yeah, yeah. I'll be all right. I'll be all right." And we'd go, "Are you sure?" and he'd go, "Oh yeah, yeah, don't worry about it. I'll be all right, youse guys. I'll be all right. Are we gonna keep on playin'?"

Then we'd start playing again, and of course down he would go again and again. God, that laughing, that spitting, that slobbering sticks in my mind. I don't know why but at the time it was funny. It was fun.

Hey, I'm not an analyst, Hooper, but this is sick. And it seems to be your first exposure to an "other." He was part of the group, but not really. He was different, not in a good way. Excuse the pun, but Chet was your whipping boy. When did this all start bugging you?

In the rehab hospital after I broke my neck.

Strange thing to be thinking about.

I know. I guess Chet was my first experience with a bona fide "other" as you call it, one of those who is somehow there but set apart. And I wish to God my memory of him—no, my memories of my attitudes toward him—were happier memories. You know what's worse?

Christ, Hooper, what other atrocities did you guys commit against this kid?

None, Spokes. But I doubt I would even be remembering Chet at all and feeling remorseful for our petty cruelties to him if I myself had not experienced a sudden, traumatic change in my life, if I myself had not, unexpectedly, become an "other."

Don't sell yourself short, Hoop. You were different long before you broke your neck and became a dreaded quad.

Ableman, must you be a smart-ass 24/7?

I must. I must. Sorry, continue Mister H.

Well, I first thought about Chet waiting for an X-ray in rehab. I was daydreaming about him. Was he merely a product of passing time, or was Chet really a haunting memory that, because of being glued to this cart, gave me my first glimpse of what it's like being different?

I don't know, Hooper, but I'm the Gene Hackman of cart-people.

What the hell is that supposed to mean, Spokes?

Well, a true cart-person is in the supine position, with their head immobilized (in my case with a neck brace), a captive ceiling watcher. If the rehab institute were turned upside down, a la the 'Poseidon Adventure,' I'll bet I could show you the way out, while everyone else would be lost looking up at the floor.

Oh, right, Spokes that sounds like a real in-demand skill.

Hey, do I make fun of your stories? Anyway, the purpose of the neck brace was to keep my head supported and straight. That, coupled with the fact that I was scared to death my head would fall off if I moved it more than a centimeter, made me a copious ceiling watcher and an expert cart-person.

Know what else?

I'm sure you'll tell me.

Cart-person waiting makes 'army-waiting' seem like a trip through a McDonald's drive-through. Cart-people are self-taught professionals of patience: experts in the monotony of biding their time.

Okay, Ableman, I concede you are the ultimate cart-person. May I continue?

Please do.

So, earlier that morning, before my 30-minute recollection of Chet, the elevator operator at rehab took a bunch of us, who couldn't push the buttons and/or ask where to be taken, to our therapy floors. Each of us had a little note, a scheduling sheet, attached to us or to our modes of transportation so the operator could take us to the right floor. As soon as we were able, we ripped that kindergarten note off and made our own pronouncement:

"Third floor. "Second floor." "Eleven."
"Where's your schedules?" The operator would ask.
"Don't know," we'd say. "It must've fallen off."

The elevator operator rolled me to the center of the lobby and announced my arrival. I caught a glimpse of someone's face as she said, "Mr. Hooper, we're going to have to move you over here against the wall *out of the way*. We'll be with you in a minute."

Out of the way! Did she say out of the way? I had not the slightest notion I was disabled, where being out of the way can, if tolerated by the individual, become a way of life. Well, at last, I thought, my turn for x-rays. Chet had faded securely into my subconscious. Suddenly, a para (paraplegic) came whipping up on two wheels, and says to the receptionist, "Hey, Judy, what's happenin'? Sorry I'm late; I'm here for my x-ray." He got right in.

Damn paras, Hoops. No manners and too much goddamned function.

Well, this one anyway. But I lost control of my circumstance.

It's different when you're unable, isn't it, Hooper?

Sure as hell is Spokes.

I had to lie there, a cart-person, unable to even flail my arms in protest and no one could hear my little voice anyway, so I opted for the more mundane activities of ceiling watching, waiting, and of course that treacherous, evil demon, thinking. Unlike the Chet memories, my typical cart-time thinking was disjunctive and self-indulging:

How did I get into such a fix?

I wonder if Bunny made it down yet?

Oh, man! Bob, Tom, Grube, Joe and I sure beat the shit out of the home office basketball team. Took 'em by 18. Forty-two points for old number six. And Grube and Bob complained I shot too much, and to this day dispute my point total, Hah!

Geez, one day I'm a sixty-minute superstar, and the next I'm a cart-person.

I wonder if Bunny made it down yet?

I was lost. And little did I know that being a cart-person was just the start. Like Frankenstein's monster, I was being brought to life as an "other." Rehab seemed so helpful then. It *was* helpful. But being different was just really beginning to squeeze my soul. I was the different one now, but in my naïveté I thought I'd be accepted as "normal" after rehab.[4]

---

4   Robin Williams committed suicide August 9, 2014. While I was in my early days of rehab, I first saw *Mork and Mindy* on the rec-room TV. It was the first time I really laughed after being injured. One of those reflexive laugh out loud laughs (before LOL became an overused acronym). I was looking around because I thought I might have been the only one who thought this guy was funny. Clearly, I wasn't. It was one of the first steps in putting me back in touch with me. Thanks Mork!

Why did I think of Chet that day? Maybe because being disabled makes you an outsider, and deep in my remorseful thoughts was a truth that I too was now "not of us." It starts some time, that feeling you fight off of being perceived and treated as different. It's a time after the initial pain and trauma, a time when you're feeling a little better, a time when you start noticing the little things that make you disabled, a time when the contemplations of your past mean something to your present. For me, my initiation into the Club Nobody Wants To Join must have started with my thoughts of Chet. At that time, disability was just a splinter from what I later realized was an entire forest of emotions.

Hey, Spokes, I found out that Chet had died a number of years ago.

I've got a message for him, Fast Eddie: If you're up there Chet, if you're up there wobbling around the streets of heaven on that beat-up bike of yours, wobble on, Jet—wobble on!

CHAPTER 3

A FATE WORSE THAN DEATH

Hooper, you had another experience with an "other" didn't you?

You know I did.

Mind rehashing that?

Well, it was 1966, I think. I had just gotten back from visiting a friend who was shot in the spine while trying to board a chopper in Vietnam. He was 20 and paralyzed from the waist down, a para. I walked in and was stunned. Jim looked skinny and broken. He was home but still recovering. I stayed for five frightening minutes and bolted out of there. I found out much later that he hadn't even remembered I'd come. I talked to him with a how's-the-weather insincerity, while seeing "cripple," thinking "cripple," and fearing that somehow I'd become a "cripple," too, if I hung around him too long. Afterwards, I sat with a couple of my buddies rendering a three-beer opinion on paralysis, and it still repeats in my thoughts like a broken record:

"I couldn't live like that."
"The poor guy's life is over."
"Man could he ever play basketball."
And the clincher: "I'd rather be in the ground than be like him."

I never went back to see Jim while I was still walking. For twelve years I avoided him, even though I'd heard he was doing well. I practiced the "out of sight, out of mind" axiom. And it was quite easy.

How complacently I'd assumed the role of my disabled friend, made my numb proclamation and walked away self-satisfied at having pronounced him dead from paralysis. Disability, I was conditioned to believe, was the end until the end: a purgatory of lameness instead of fire.

So, Hoop, you never heard from him again?

Not exactly, Spokes.

Twelve-plus years later, an emotional conflict was raging in my non-disabled mind, tenuously affixed to my now-disabled body. I wanted to be "normal." I wanted to be Ed Hooper again—God, how I wanted to be normal again. Rehab was synonymous with pain and paralysis, and I cringed at its daily reminders: the therapy, the blood mobile, the medication, and the struggling patients. But I also felt protected inside rehab. It protected me from an outside world I conjured up, filled with pointing fingers, dreadful whispers and woeful stares. Rehab's walls hurt, but they were safe. (More in Chapter Twelve).

It was time. I had been going home for several weekends. My neck brace was off. I was ready. But I resisted any opportunity to meet the real world on *its* own turf, to face all those bogey-people—those freaking "normals." My sister-in-law Connie's wedding was coming up, out of town. Cindy was going to be matron of honor. Since she was the only person outside rehab who had any experience caring for me, we decided I would go back and stay at rehab that weekend, freeing Cindy up to attend the wedding. I figured this was the best solution. Otherwise, I'd be just an added burden, *in the way*. I checked back in at rehab and spent the morning brooding. Later in the day Cindy would be leaving town for the wedding. Anna, one of the rehab nurses I'd been able to confide in, saw me pouting (as I'd hoped she would) and came over to talk. I hadn't wanted to be a bother to Cindy, I told her. I didn't want to cause a fuss that might ruin the wedding.

"Ed, why don't you call Cindy and tell her that you want to go?" Anna asked.

"I don't want to go," I whined. "It's all just too much trouble." I wanted to go so badly I could have spit corsages.

"Call her," Anna gently insisted. "It's obvious you want to go, and you're using your condition as an easy way out. Call her, Ed."

Oh, sure, I thought, call her. What was I going to say? I felt as though I'd be doing something wrong if I called Cindy. I felt the rush of blood behind my eyes, the flood of warm confusion you feel when you're working up the courage to ask your first girl out on a date. But this was my wife! Anna was right, though. Cindy would understand. All I wanted to do was go to Connie's wedding. It was so simple. It was so hard. Finally, I asked Anna to dial the number.

Anna handed me the phone. Trembling now, I said, "Hi, Babe, it's me. I got to thinking about Connie's wedding and, uh, I want, I want ... " Suddenly, I burst into tears—tears pumping up from where I'd been storing them since early that morning. Bawling now, short of breath, my nose running, my eyes swelling from crying, I finished my plea. "I want to go with you," I sputtered.

Naturally, Cindy came down to get me, and we were off to the wedding.

Cindy was busy with rehearsals so I just hung around her parents' house. On the day of the wedding, my brother came over to stay with me. I'd decided I wasn't feeling too well that afternoon (acute, frightened anxiety disorder), so I opted for making the reception afterward as my re-introduction to the real world. Don and I watched football on TV and shot the breeze while everyone else attended the wedding. Evening rolled around, and it was time for the reception.

Ok, I thought, time for the old Ed Hooper, time for Fast Eddie to show his "cool." In rolled Mr. Party, Mr. Gregarious, Mr. Cool. Mister Wreck!

I was wheeled to a convenient spot out of the way of traffic and dancing. A voice squeezing and ripping at my chest kept insisting, "Slow Eddie, get the hell out of here." But I didn't. I sat with my mother and Andy my stepfather.

I could feel the whole world feasting on my crippledness. I had Andy get me a beer in hopes it would depress the anxiety. It didn't. I tried another, with the same result. The voices were all too clear in my head:

"There's Ed, that poor bastard."

"Oh, isn't he the young man who was crippled in that car wreck?"

"Drinking and driving, wasn't it?"

"Too bad. He seemed like such a vital young man."

"His whole life was ahead of him."

"It just goes to show you how quickly it can all end."

Some friends and a few of the family came over. Not that many people, really, but I felt swarmed with kisses and voices. Kisses: on my lips, my cheeks, my forehead. Being told how nice I looked. I didn't feel like I looked nice. I didn't have a clue what I looked like, but I was damn sure I didn't look good. I still hadn't looked at myself since breaking my neck because my mirror was a dark alley. I was afraid to go near it, afraid of what I'd find in there. CRIPPLE would lunge out and mug my mind.

The moment cinched around me like a noose. I wanted out. Why had I even come? Please, I thought, keep these people away from me! Cripples, stay home out of the way! You're broken furniture, defective goods. Stay home! I wanted to take their kisses and pity and cloak them with my self-pity and disappear like a mist into the cool November night.

The voices ricocheted in my head until I couldn't distinguish between what I was hearing and what I had imagined. The words rang with clarity because I, at one time, had been one of those voices myself and said more, much more. I knew the words because I said those same words myself. And, yes, I had laughed at, scoffed at, pitied or ignored the "different ones": The fat, the slow, the lame, the clumsy, the ones not quite "with it." The voices I heard were my own. I was "a fate worse than death"—at a wedding no less. I could cope better with my loss than I could handle those discreet looks and whispers I knew so well. I met the cripple and he was me.

I languished at the reception for a little more than an hour. Finally I asked to leave. I was wheeled out amid whispers:

"Is Ed all right?"

"He's going already?"

"Oh, my! He looks a little pale."

My mother explained, "Oh, he's just a bit tired," as Andy wheeled me away. "It's his first time out," she said. (No, Ma! I screamed inside myself. I just can't take this for one more second).

Ah, the waiting car: its safety greeted me. It hid me so well!

I went back to rehab with my tail between my legs.

One day not long after the wedding, "Telephone for you, Ed," Anna, the nurse, said to me.

"Hi. Is this Eddie Hopper?" The voice asked. It sounded vaguely familiar. A friend might say "Hopper" instead of "Hooper," I thought. But I couldn't pin the voice to a person.

"Who's this?" I asked.

"Jim Bump. How ya doin'?"

He, of course, is the same Jim who I visited twelve years earlier. We talked for a good while, and without intruding, he offered his help after I got out of rehab.

In a wholly different way than Chet, Jim was now a more meaningful part of my past. Had I not been injured myself, Jim Bump would have been tucked away in my subconscious. Now, I was having a shameful recollection of this man who called to ask how I was doing. I was pretty much wrong about everything, but this was just the beginning of my long road to meaningful recovery.

It's been years since Jim's unforgettable phone call, but I am still amazed how different our two after-injury visits were—how different our "how are you doing" questions were. My words were only defenses to shroud my own fear. His, though, were a way of reaching out with empathy. He knew what I learned later: there's a fellowship (not to be confused with friendship) to be discovered in disability. It took me a while to come around, but Jim and I know two things about one another: We live with our disabilities, and, yes, we are friends.

Jim had been happy for years, but I'd never had guts enough to find out. I wonder how many "friends" run scared like I did—never seeing disabled people for who and what they really are: full human beings.

Jeez, Hooper, you certainly had your head screwed on crooked. That first time out is the hardest though. We try so hard to be our old selves, but the change is drastic; the old you is not who you are anymore, and there is no quick fix to make you feel "normal," to become the new you.

Yeah, Spokes, I was pathetic.

No, Hoop, you were normal for where you were on your journey.

I guess.

Hoop, that wedding didn't totally suck for you. Do you remember what your little nephew Chad did?

Oh, that's right. He grabbed the vertical projections on my hand rims, and rolled the wheelchair back and forth. He looked like a miniature riverboat captain at the wheel of his paddleboat.

Yep, no voices, no prejudice—just a 3-year-old boy who hadn't yet learned the words.

It's a long road, Hooper, from back then to where you and I finally arrived. Not to toot my own horn too loud, but I'm curious what happened to you that brought my fabulous self to the surface.

Give me a break, Ableman.

CHAPTER 4

APHASIA

"Babe, would you geth the egllaatrr buttton? Boy, I must really be beat."

Cindy and I took the elevator up to physical therapy. By the time we arrived, an incredible imploding feeling was overwhelming me. I'd lost my source of language. My world was shrinking as if I were falling into a deep well, with my wife's face at the top, getting smaller and smaller. Through the smallness and dimness I could see the panic wrenched on her face.

I'd been saying things like, "raghhitttifrmmdgg, son-of-a-bitchin' fucker, sssxazzuttt." I could cuss with tutored clarity, but the rest was nonsense to everyone else. Only I could understand. I could hear my love's frightened voice, "Please, don't try to ask anything. Don't talk. Rest. Stay quiet, please, please."

"Ghrrappl drrrddippll cccoppykk?" I wanted to know what was going on.

My head was a can of alphabet soup overstocked with consonants. Gibberish spilled out of my mouth with every r, d and t shaking my wife Cindy to the bone.

Cindy and a couple of therapists had stepped outside the partition for a moment, and I could hear their frantic whispers: "Get a blood pressure cuff! I think he's had a stroke!"

Nooooooooooo!" My fall was now at light speed. No please, oh, please, no; no, not a stroke," I pleaded within myself.

A neurologist was waiting for me on the medical floor. "Can you count to ten?" He asked me.

"Four, two, nniii... " I responded.

"Who is the president of the United States?"

My brain was a pinball machine. Amid the clanging and clatter, I kept waiting for TILT or Game Over. There was a disconnection of thought and language, and I squirmed and struggled for what could have been a month with the answer I wanted. Then, "Peanuts. Peanuts. Peanuts. No! Fucking Son-of-a-bitch! Goddamnit! No, peanuts, no, no ... "

Then the neurologist pulled the plug on me: "What is your wife's name?"

"Mary!" I blurted. "Noooo!"

God, I'd called Cindy "Mary." The mental implosion was complete: I was trapped in a black hole of the mind.

Cindy was at my bedside as she was every single day. Her face faded and cleared; faded and cleared, faded... She was trying to comfort me; but calling her Mary wasn't reassuring either of us. I had a horrible headache and was asking Cindy (calling her Mary) for some Tylenol, but I had the letters jumbled like an anagram, so when it finally came out it sounded like, Nellyt. Naturally, she couldn't understand, which only served to infuriate me. God damn Nellyt! Nellyt! God-damn, son-of-a-bitchin' bastard!

My swearing soon turned to crying, and Cindy's eyes were red with tears, too.

Around then my mother arrived and I overhead her talking to Cindy. "There's not much you can do," she said. "You're probably going to have to put him in a nursing home."

"Ma, stop, what the fuck are you saying," I thought. "Not the dreaded nursing home. I'm in here. Someone come find me." But of course I couldn't say anything understandable. My mind was asking if this was how it would end, here in the rehab hospital, in the solitary darkness of my thoughts, my wife and mother looking on helplessly?

I fell asleep. Around 3 a.m., the nurse came in and asked me, "Who is the President?"

"Jimmy Carter? Jimmy Carter! Jimmy Carter!"

Oh, God, I thought. 1,2,3,4,5,6,7,8,9,10. Two times four is eight. Four times eight is thirty-two. A hundred, a thousand, ten thousand. Oh, baby! Walter Mondale! Gerry Ford! "Go tell Cindy! GO TELL CINDY!"

A week or two after my aphasia nightmare (caused by an antibiotic) I got another look at it. Irene, a "stroke patient," had aphasia and took physical therapy the same hours I did. Therapists at rehab had to do a lot of doubling and tripling with patients. Time's money, you know.

Irene worked very hard in therapy. I was amazed at what she'd accomplished. She was doing it all: bed, bath, in and out of her wheelchair, starting to walk a little, on and off the toilet. I'd presumed her occupational therapy was going well, too.

Irene was quiet. Aphasia did that. It made her understand that others didn't understand; so silence, in Irene's case, was a method of dealing with her frustration. But she followed instructions like a trooper. I now realize I'm prouder of her in retrospect because in rehab, I was always secretly envious of those who could do more than I could.

Irene's husband and son came to visit her often, and I was happy the day I heard she'd be going home soon. But a few days later, I encountered her in therapy crying, and refusing to do any therapy. She was headed for a nursing home. She had not had a voice in her fate, though she'd spoken clearly through her actions and her many accomplishments that she was ready to resume life at home, her own home.

I overheard her husband talking to the doctor and therapist:

"She doesn't understand a word I say. How can I care for her?"

"She understands you," the therapist insisted, as if she'd said it many times before. "Try to be patient with her. Help her."

"Home is the best place for Irene," the doctor firmly told her husband. "It will give her an environment conducive to recovery."

"It's easy for you people," Irene's husband was protesting. "You don't have to take care of her day and night. I work. I can't. I'm sorry."

That's all I heard. All, except the painful sobbing of Irene. It was a lonely cry, so much like the loneliness I'd felt, ever so briefly, weeks earlier. I knew she was trapped inside herself, with tears the only residual of her hope. I never heard what happened to Irene. I hope she didn't die lonely.

Holy crap, Hooper, stop. I need a break.

Sadly, aphasia gives no breaks. It is a devastating disability. It envelops the mind, giving it no access to the outside world. In this way, it renders the person devoid of any way of calling out for their rights or articulating what they want. Eventually, without support and understanding, a person with aphasia simply loses hope.

Often, we with disabilities get treated like we have aphasia. Our words are heard as gibberish outside of our own circles. It's as though we're making sense only within ourselves. Society hears it as so much gobbledygook.

How many times can we say it, ask it, scream it—that we're ok, that we do not want pity?

How long, Spokes, how long before even a tiny bit of what we know to be true will be understood as something more than nonsense?

Does never sound too long to you, Fast Eddie? Remove thy head from thy ass, my man. How many times have you tried to explain this shit, only to be greeted by a blank face of confusion?

Spokes, ever the optimist. We must continue to talk to other people with disabilities. We have brothers and sisters who really do understand disability—that is common purpose, man.

Hoops, are you on some kind of mind-altering drugs? Supposedly there are 40+ million disabled folks gimping around our country. Well, someone better tell 30 to 40 million of 'em that they're disabled because they don't have a clue. If you use a wheelchair, try going up to someone with a hearing aid, and telling him that you're both in the same community. Good freakin' luck!

Yeah, I know. Recently I had lunch with a friend who has diabetes, and rheumatoid arthritis so severe that he can hardly walk. He told me about all of his symptoms and his ordeals. I said, yeah it can be tough adjusting to disability. He said, "I don't know how you've done it all these years. I would have killed myself."

Jesus, Hooper, doesn't he know how insulting that is?

I guess not, Spokes. It's what he's learned. He is still walking which seems to be the common yardstick when it comes to how disabled one is. In his head, he was doing really badly, but it could have been far worse. He could be like me.

Slap!

You know, even now, after all these years, we have no sense of community. There's the Gay Community, the Black Community, the woman's movement, the Immigration Movement, and on and on. But where is the Disability Community?

Let's not forget the bowel movement.

Spokes, please. Take a break.

What, the shitty end of the stick has no appeal to you?

No, but if we had a sense of community, we could be there for one another.

We were closer to that reality twenty years ago than we are now, Hooper.

It's true. Where's our NAACP or NOW or our Rainbow? Where's our magazine that speaks directly to us? At least we had the *Disability Rag* back in the day. For those newly disabled, where can they go? Who can they talk to? Who will be there with the credibility to say hang in there? Who'll be there to say to someone who is suffering that it will be all right?

On the flipside, so much positive has happened in terms of accessibility and inclusion, but there is no sense of community for us. What's needed is a philosophy we can share. Not a "how to," but a "who"— who we are beneath our gimpy, deaf, blind, deformed, amputated, retarded, crippled selves.

Alone, each of us could easily end up like Irene, trapped within ourselves. Our journey should tell you it doesn't need to be that way. Sure I had plenty of help, still do, and there's plenty of help out there. You just need to search a lot harder today to find it. There are pockets of help within support groups, but there is no source that deals with the philosophy of disability and what it means. To forge a unity of thought, we must vigorously acknowledge disability to ourselves, or we will never be acknowledged.

CHAPTER 5

THE OUTSIDER'S PARADOX

Ok, Hoop, so you got out of rehab and you're looking for work. What then?

Well, Spokes, it really came to a head with a conversation I had with Dunsmore Priggé...

"Hello, Mr. Priggé, this is Ed again. We've talked about this a dozen times: Has the company decided when I can come back and give work a try?

"I'm ready. I know I can only do deskwork, but I'd be a real asset to the company in that position. I mean, with all the years of experience I've had— well, it can only help in dealing with customers."

"And we really want you back," my old boss said. "But there are internal problems."

"Like what?" I asked.

"Well, like salary. What would we pay you?"

"I'll work for the minimum wage, for nothing, just to prove to you all that I can do the job. Then we can talk about money. I just want the chance."

"We've got legal problems, too," he said. "What if you were to fall? Who'd be responsible? The company is worried about this."

"They're worried about me falling?" I asked, surprised. "Christ, man, I've already fallen. I'm paralyzed and in a wheelchair. Besides, after my injury, I made a point of keeping the lawyers out of the company's business. I made sure no legal action was taken against them. I'm not coming after anyone," not actually saying what we both knew: that I was drinking at an office retirement party the night I was injured.

"What's the real problem here?" I asked.

"Ed, the company has consulted its attorneys, and that's the information that's been fed back to me."

"You mean that's it? I can't even work for nothin'? I've been at this, one way or another for six months! All the phone calls, all the letters, all the waiting, for what? Man, I don't understand this!"

"Sorry," said Priggé.

"Yeah ..." I said goodbye as the phone hit the receiver.

Dunsmore Priggé was only sorry when his butt was in the wringer. Priggé was mostly concerned with Priggé. So my friends, who were lobbying to get me back to work, had convinced him that I would be the perfect choice to handle the sales desk. That would free him to play golf, or whatever the hell else he was up to when he'd disappear for entire afternoons, sometimes an entire day.

The problem was that, within the company, Priggé had the political weight of a helium-filled balloon. He was my only chance to work in my old office. In the end, that was no chance at all. I made plans to sell my two-story, inaccessible house, leave the city, and move back to my hometown. It's a small town and the headquarters of my pre-disability employer.

I decided I'd make a direct appeal for a job to the company's sales manager, Charles Coldwell.

"Hi, Mr. Coldwell. This is Ed Hooper. I'll be moving down in June and was wondering about starting work on the inside desk." I was hopeful.

"We've been over all this with Dunsmore," he said. "The company doesn't have much to offer you."

"I worked for you for ten years. I made nearly $40,000 the year I was injured, with 1979 looking to go up to $60,000. I never had a down year. God knows how much I've made for the company. Doesn't that mean something?" I asked, remembering all the talk of the company as "family." ($40,000 is roughly $143,000 in 2015 money)[5]

"Of course it does, Ed. But it was your job to make money for us. Can you write longhand yet?"

"Yes," I answered, taken aback by the question.

"That's good," he muttered. "But to be perfectly honest with you I don't see what I, ah, we can do."

"Okay." I hung up.

Good grief, I thought, Coldwell is the man who once told me, "Never believe anyone who feels he must tell you how honest he's being."

---

5   United States Department of Labor, Bureau of Labor Statistics Inflation Calculator

What had happened, I wondered? Before I broke my neck, Charles Coldwell was one of my strongest supporters. What was going on? I knew everyone was expendable: corporate Dixie cups. But there was more going on here than my corporate mortality. I wasn't even being given an opportunity to prove my worth. What had happened to the assurances I'd been given right after my injury? Coldwell's words from a year earlier—"You'll always have a job here, Ed"—rang like a dull, shallow bell in my mind.

A friend told me that all Coldwell and the others can remember is my lying helplessly on a striker frame with bolts screwed into the sides of my head. They thought I was worthless.

Perhaps I am, I thought.

But work was my way of proving to the world that I was "normal." If that were taken away, the grim reality of being a "cripple" would have to be faced. I couldn't quit. Not yet.

We moved back to my hometown. On advice from an old working buddy, I phoned Samuel Grey, chief executive officer of the company.

"Mr. Grey," I asked, "can I come down to your home and discuss the possibility of my working for the company again?"

"Yes, of course, you can, Ed."

Several days later, I went down to meet with him. After the social amenities, I began by saying, "Mr. Grey, you know why I'm here. I want an opportunity to work. My worth is in my experience and training: I know the product; I've been selling it for ten years; I've handled large and complex customer accounts. And you know I'm willing to work hard."

"True, Ed," Grey acknowledged, "but there are factors here that the board members and I have discussed since you've called. This may sound weird, even anti-American, but you made *too much money* as a salesman. And I don't see how we can justify paying you the equivalent of what you now make on Social Security and disability insurance benefits."

"I knew that would be a problem, Sam. I also know I could probably go on a trial work period from Social Security for awhile. So is the government or the insurance company interested in offering me any kind of subsidy until I can see if I can earn enough to maintain my standard-of-living?" I asked.

"You're kidding, right, Ed? The government is a dinosaur in these matters and insurance companies are sharks. Either way, they won't work with you by way of a subsidy."

"In other words," I said, "all these people are interested in when you talk to them about working is getting the recipients off their ledgers."

"That's about it, Ed."

"What are you getting from them now?" he asked.

"I get 60% of the $40,000 or $24,000 a year," I replied ($86,000 in 2015 money)[6]. "But that's virtually tax free; it's like getting $35,000 gross income. My insurance premiums are waived, too," I told him.

"Ed, we could never pay you that kind of money for inside desk work. It would be unfair to other employees who do the same kind of work. You understand that don't you?"

---

6 United States Department of Labor, Bureau of Labor Statistics Inflation Calculator

"No, Sam, I don't understand. I'm a trained expert in this field. I was thinking that my services would be thought of more in a managerial sense. And just to have the job, I'd take $25,000 a year."

"I don't know. It doesn't look workable," Grey said. He seemed genuinely sorry about the apparent impasse.

"I'll start out slowly, and we can see how I fit in," I told him.

Then I just asked: "Whaddya say, Sam? A chance?"

"Okay, Ed, provided the board and other executives agree."

"Fair enough," I said, realizing I could still sell. But why was it so difficult, I thought?

We looked at one another, both suspecting my frustration and disappointment would be the inevitable product of this agreement with one major difference: Grey thought I would fail outright; I thought I would succeed—and lose all I'd fought for because I wouldn't be able to earn enough money to provide for my family.

Though $25,000 was, in effect, a $10,000 ($36,000 in 2015 money)[7] cut in pay, I felt it was worth the loss in dollars for the gain in self-esteem. What was this obsession that allowed me to sacrifice $10,000 in yearly security for my wife and two children?

Cindy could get a job, I figured, and we'd work our way back financially.

I had to interview with the very same people I'd worked with for ten years. Four company executives attended the interview: Sam Grey, Charles Coldwell, Frank Hawkins, and Lyle Stillman.

---

7   United States Department of Labor, Bureau of Labor Statistics Inflation Calculator

"Can you write?" asked Coldwell.

"Yes, with a felt-tipped pen."

"Can you show us?" Hawkins asked.

I took a felt tip pen, and, sitting sideways to the desk, scribbled out my name. A 2-year-old could have done as well. They all looked at me as if to say, "Christ, man, you can't even write your own name!"

"I do better when I'm straight to the desk using my own pen. Besides, I'll be using the dictating machine for most of my work." I didn't come prepared for this, I thought.

"What about your ability to take notes over the phone?" Hawkins queried.

"I can do it."

"Are you sure?"

"Yes! I'm sure. And I'll get better."

"Can you get files from the drawers?"

"No. But... ah, the file clerk gets everyone's files. Yours too, right?

Damn! I thought I was finished. In desperation I blathered, "I can shave myself with a straight razor."

"What?" They all asked simultaneously. "A straight razor?"

"No, no, I mean a safety razor. I mean, ah... I don't use an electric razor." I was losing control. Just laugh, Hooper, I told myself, and get a grip on the situation. I laughed. They joined me—little, polite laughs. It was all quite odd. I knew each of these men well, but we were all acting as if I were a different person. It was like Ed Hooper was a memory, and a strange, helpless man was being interviewed.

This was a session of "can't do's," and I was sick of explaining the obvious. My reason for being there was to discuss what I could do. I explained my qualifications and ideas to them as I had to Mr. Grey in his home.

"What about pay?" Mr. Grey asked.

"I'll work for the minimum wage until you can decide if I'm worth keeping. I have a nine-month-trial work period. Before that time expires, everyone will know if I'm worth a further investment.

Am I hired?" I knew I had to ask then, or my chance might have been lost.

"Yes," Grey said.

Coldwell, Hawkins, and Stillman looked as if to say, "Sam, you have got to be kidding."

I'm sure I was hired because of my persistence and out of pity. No one in that room, other than me, thought a quadriplegic could do the job. But I could have cared less about their attitudes. I had the job I'd dreamed about from the early days of my injury, through the rigors of rehab, and through the intense lobbying campaign my friends and I had mounted these last months.

Reality soon diminished my celebration. In one year, I'd gone from being a $40,000 per year traveling industrial salesman, to a $3.35 per hour trainee. Within my nine-month trial work period, how could I possibly convince these same people to pay me $25,000 a year?

As I left, I asked myself: Why should I pursue something so frustrating? I'd ask myself that many times. The answer had always been the same: Hope. I believed I could prove myself, and justify the company paying me at least $25,000 per year, maybe more.

Sixteen months had passed since I'd broken my neck after an office party. But I was back at work and ready to prove myself to the skeptics at the company.

Initially, I was treated like a trainee. I handled routine phone calls, routine follow-ups on orders, and routine pricing. I knew I could never succeed in the rut of mediocrity. To have any chance of convincing those "you've got to be kidding for hiring Hooper" faces, I had to work with the vital customer accounts and handle them much better than any other "desk man." I would, I reasoned, document my successes, and use that record to negotiate for a contract.

Coldwell was my key, and he and I both knew it. He was sales manager, and his favorable recommendation was critical to me getting the job I wanted. Unfortunately, Coldwell's ego was bigger than the company's plant, and my ideas as to how I'd fit in were little more than static between the serenades he heard from his own voice.

One day Coldwell was explaining to me his thoughts on working: "I started here forty years ago, at the bottom." He began every company story the same way. "Stan used to work in the sample room. He had polio, ya know. He could walk, but was crippled-up pretty bad. Smart guy. Well, ol' Stan worked for twenty-five years making samples and brochures for us and was always proud of his work. He still calls, now and then, and tells me how grateful he is that I gave him a job.

"I think you have to know your capabilities, Ed, and learn to deal with what life metes out. When Stan retired a few years ago, they hired Jimmy, that retarded kid. He's okay, I guess.

"You knew Stan, didn't you?" Coldwell looked at me.

"Yeah, I knew him, a very nice man." What the hell was this guy talking about, I wondered. Was he telling me how to be disabled? Did he think just being here is enough? I was after a $25,000 a year job, and he was equating my situation with the sample man. And if he saw Stan as all "crippled-up," how must he see me? He somehow thought that my disability affected my mind and skills—that the more disabled I was, the less I could do, and I was pretty freaking disabled.

I'd decided there were two major obstacles in my way of success. (Really there were three, but I didn't learn about the third until later.) The first was the company's rigid management structure, which dated back 80 years. They were successful in that system and weren't going to be easily swayed into creating a middle management position that would justify them paying me $25,000 a year.

The second was that I was a "cripple." No one was so crass as to say it—except for Coldwell's thoughtless, biased anecdote—but we all knew it, even me. That was what I had to overcome, I figured, in order to succeed.

I worked insufferably hard trying to "overcome" being a "cripple." It's what I now call The Outsider's Paradox: You strive so hard to be "normal" that you appear abnormal. At the company, inside desk people didn't like either the attention or the salaries paid to outside sales people. This envy produced some unproductive friction within the sales department, and, as prejudices do, spread to other departments in the company. I had worked both sides of the fence, and saw this as a problem that was costing the company money.

So I began my quest for permanent employment by treating the outside salesmen like something more than greedy bastards in three-piece suits; and they responded by coming to me with their large accounts. I was solving big problems, working on big orders, big accounts, and substantiating that I was what every company yearns for: a profit-maker.

I documented my more prestigious successes, and put the initials of Grey, Coldwell, Hawkins, and Stillman on those files. God, those eight months went fast. I never called in sick a single day. I think everyone in the office thought of me as "normal." It felt good being treated normally—being accepted as Ed Hooper again. I'd stopped working to be myself—I simply was myself. It felt right.

When you're disabled, though, normalcy seems to always come with compromise. Because the rest rooms were inaccessible, I had a friend empty my urine collecting leg bag. With my head down, I went to a corner of the office where she'd empty it into a plastic container for disposal.

Hooper, stop, STOP! I can't take this for one more second. You pissed out in the middle of an office with 15 people watching and you thought that was ok? That's not normal, man.

Spokes, this was before I met you. I thought because I was the "handicapped" one, I was the one who had to adjust, to give up my privacy, bow my head and accept this indignity to have a job and to be "normal." What is repugnant to me, in retrospect, is that I didn't complain one bit.

You sure as hell should have. Sorry for interrupting, but, shit you didn't have to endure this. No one does.

I thought I did, Spokes.

Anyway, I slowed my intake of liquids to reduce my number of trips to the office corner. There was no ramp, so I was also carried up and down the stairs to get in and out of the building, until I found a back way in through the plant. I never complained. I'd been assured that everything would be "corrected" if I were hired permanently.

I had one month left on my trial work period. It was time to gather all my accomplishments, all my wits, and all my savvy to sell myself to these skeptics one more time.

I really had a chance! I figured.

I met with Coldwell first. "Well, Chuck," I said, "my trial time is about up. Nothing's really changed since I was hired insofar as what kind of money I need to provide for my family."

"Ed, I started here forty years ago, at the bottom, and worked my way through the ranks," Coldwell began. "You've surprised me; you really have. I'd like to see you stay on as a desk man at say $15,000 a year."

"That's not gonna work," I said. He knows that, I thought.

"I think," Coldwell said, after a pause, "that you have to accept what's been dealt to you by life. Sell your house. Get a smaller home or rent. Learn to live with less. You won't regret it in 10 or 15 years when having a job will mean everything to you."

"What?!" I was incredulous. You know I need $25,000, and your recommendation to the board to stay on here," I explained, puzzled and angered by his perversity or inability to understand that I paid for insurance and Social Security to protect my family financially in case of an unexpected disability.

"Ed, Priggé said he'd like you back to your old office. Maybe we could work something out there," Coldwell suggested.

"It's 1980," I responded. "The bottom is out of the housing market. You know I can't move back there. I need your help," I reiterated, glancing at the Wall Street Journal on his desk. Hell, he knew I couldn't sell my home for a fair price and move again!

"Well, I don't see what more I can offer," Coldwell finished matter-of-factly. "Go to Sam Grey. He's the man who hired you."

So that was his problem, I thought. He thinks I back-doored him. No, that can't be it, I reasoned; I went through him to get to Grey. Jesus, why won't this man help me? Was it still the wheelchair? I asked myself as I rolled out of Coldwell's office.

I went to see Sam Grey.

"Sam, I've got documentation here of new customers I've gotten, and the fact that I'm directly responsible for saving two large accounts that we were in danger of losing. Here, look at these numbers." I shoved the files toward him. "I've saved the company ... "

"Ed," he interrupted, "I don't dispute your numbers, but there's an old business axiom: if you don't do it someone else will. I know you've done a fine job, but if you weren't here, if I wasn't here, someone else would pick up the slack. There's no need to show me your figures."

"Come on, Sam. You know that people *do* make a difference. Some do a much better job than others, and that accounts are kept and lost by good management and often lost by management blunders. Come on."

"Sorry, Ed. We've done the best we can do."

I almost felt like begging, but I couldn't go that low.

"I've got a letter coming to you outlining my proposal," I muttered, knowing it was no use; I'd be gone in a week or two.

"I'm sorry, Ed. Really sorry." He seemed sincere; he always did.

I was offered $21,000 a year with full benefits. (Sam Grey's work, I concluded.) There would be no new position, though. And I was offered the same desk job, which held little chance for advancement.

My friends and fellow employees came up with numerous covert ploys to fool the payers of my disability insurance into thinking I wasn't working. The ideas ranged from hand delivered cash payments to paying a relative, which would hide my identity as the real "wage-earner." Some ideas were quite appealing: I could've worked at full salary and collected benefits as well. But the schemes were, of course, illegal. The ideas were alluring, though, because they all carried with them an ironic kind of justice by screwing the screwers. Of course, I didn't.

I went back to see Sam Grey to explain.

"Sam, I appreciate the effort you made and the offer (I really didn't appreciate it one bit), but after some checking, I've discovered that, even with an optimistic tax refund, I'd take home around $15,000 to $16,000 a year. That's a loss of $8,000 to $9,000 ($25,000 to $30,000 in 2015 dollars)[8] per year to my family and me.

"I understand." Grey said. "I wish I could help."

In an agonizing decision, I concluded the differential in pay was too great; they couldn't pay me what I needed, so I resigned.

---

8   United States Department of Labor, Bureau of Labor Statistics Inflation Calculator

Shortly after I left the company, I found out Coldwell's son-in-law was being hired as an inside deskman. He was being groomed for a higher-paying position. Today he is the company sales manager. It worked out quite well for him, and, in the end, it worked out great for me too. I didn't know it then, but had I gotten the job, I would have been stuck in a small town that would have stifled me. So, I begrudge no one anything.

These maneuvers are quite common in business. But this move was particularly insidious. Coldwell's motives had nothing to do with my disability, yet absolutely everything; he used my disability like a sharp tool to his ultimate advantage. He just sat back and watched me, struggling for acceptance, fearing the tentacles of government or insurance would strangle me if I went near them for help. He saw me worrying (because the system wouldn't help) about the future of my wife and children. He fed me his beliefs. He wanted me to see myself as he did, a cripple with no potential or real future so that his son-in-law, who was able-bodied, could step in. And it worked.

At some level I believed that bullshit, too. This job was all that I was trained for, and although confident, I thought, maybe I really was too handicapped to be an executive, and after a pretty good fight I failed. Realistically, it was either sell my house and have my family suffer, or resign. I resigned. Coldwell, that third, unknown obstacle, was the instrument of my unemployment.

As time healed my wounded dreams, I understood that Coldwell, although misguided and mistaken, wasn't the real problem. Yes, he stood by and watched—with some mental pangs, I hope—the system at work. He couldn't unlearn in eight months what he spent a lifetime learning.

So I collected every nickel of my benefits knowing I did my best. But when someone asks me if I'm working hard, I get a latent screwed feeling.

Although I do work hard now, that question dredges up some bittersweet memories. So I cock my head, smile, and say, "Working…? Hardly."

May I summarize, Hooper: You kissed their asses and they handed you yours.

Oh, Spokes, I forgot to tell you that during my trial work period the life insurance carrier the company used canceled my policy saying I wasn't disabled enough to qualify for waivers.

What!? You're a freaking quad, an-all-four-limbs, wheelchair-using quad. One doesn't get too much more disabled than that.

The company fixed it somehow with some wheeling dealing. I never really cared how.

What a benevolent bunch of dickheads.

Spokes, they really didn't know any better. Like I said, it's what they had learned their entire lives.

That's crap, Hooper. People once believed that the earth was the center of the universe. Some still do. But when someone demonstrated that it was round and orbited the sun, people saw the proof and said, 'Hey, this Copernicus dude is really on to something.'

Your old company didn't help when you needed it most, Hoop. You're not unlike Irene in the previous chapter. You showed you could do it, but it didn't matter to them. Hell, that $4,000 differential in pay was a drop in the bucket to the company, but it was everything to you. And they knew it.

They couldn't see this gimp, this quad, this pathetic cripple as a viable executive in their company. So they chose to ignore your accomplishments, and, what's far worse, ultimately used your disability against you, making them far more defective than you will ever be, my friend.

Know what else, Fast Eddie?

I'm sure you'll tell me.

They did you a favor. Best damn thing that ever happened to you.

It certainly didn't feel that way, Ableman.

I know, but much bigger and much better things were coming your way. You didn't like small-town living to begin with. You wouldda been stuck there.

Christ, Hooper, I hope your next step is a little cheerier.

Not really, Spokes.

CHAPTER 6

THE BIRTH OF SPOKES ABLEMAN

It was regroup time. I was again lost after the work debacle.

I'd been disabled for nearly three years, but I didn't think I was like other "handicapped" people. Sure, I used a wheelchair, but I was, well, "normal." My friends were all "normal," too—they could walk, see, hear, and speak. I didn't want my life screwed up any further by hanging around "the handicapped."

I had enrolled in the local college. After getting a "handicapped parking sticker" for my van, I was shown "the handicapped" parking area: two spaces, on a hill, marked "special." Adjacent was the administrators' parking, on level ground. As one can easily imagine, wheelchairs do best on flat surfaces. Hills are hazardous, the steeper the hill the greater the danger.

The "handicapped" entrance was through the biology lab's greenhouse. There were two doors, one four feet beyond the other, inaccessible to those of us with limited hand function. For a year, I, along with seven or eight other people with disabilities, accepted this as the price we paid for being "handicapped." Our attitude was: we can get in and attend classes and get educated, so what do we have to gripe about?

Inside the doors, a concrete tunnel greeted us. The Tunnel wormed around the perimeter of the building. It led to everything from the biology lab, to the machine shop, to the storage areas, to the boiler room. It even had an office or two along the way. At the start of The Tunnel, to the right, was a ramp that only Conan the Wheelchair-user would attempt to conquer. The ramp's slope must be in the 20 to 25-degree range. Steeeeep!

I needed assistance going both up and down. Up was okay. Down was terror! It would have turned into a thrill ride if my helper's hands ever slipped or the handle grips came off. The Tunnel turned to the right at the bottom, so a concrete wall would have awaited my frantic arrival.

Hey, Hoop, you would have become a beautiful gimp mural, framed in chrome and spokes, on the concrete wall below. You still had your able-bodied brain spinning inside, didn't you?

Yeah, I thought this was all up to me.

Anyway, at the top of the ramp was an elevator that ran up to the main floor where the nondisabled—a.k.a. able-bodied—students went in and out of the building.

One night in The Tunnel changed everything.

Bunny and I attended night classes together. She was studying to become a nurse. One night, running late, and with only a third of The Tunnel's lights lit, we made our way out of the elevator at the machine shop, into The Tunnel, past the caged white rats waiting for psychology experiments, down 60 yards of eerie tunnel gloom, up a manageable ramp, around two corners to the so-called access door.

It was cold, so Cindy went ahead to warm up the van and lower the lift.

The access door shut behind her. Shut and locked. The whole college was locked. This was before cell phones, and I was a little scared of the dark.

Of course you were, Hooper.

Hey, clam up, Ableman, it was spooky in there.

So, I tried to open the door from the inside. It was a one-way lock, but I couldn't get both my hands on the slippery round metal doorknob. I turned and faced The Tunnel. "Is anyone here?" I yelled.

"Anybody here?" I shouted again. Nothing but silence greeted me from the dimly lit tunnel.

I knew Cindy could go to a phone and call someone, and eventually I would get out. But I felt caged.

After a half hour or so looking and shouting for help, I went back to the door a final time. Cindy was waiting. I spit all over the palm of my right hand, and, hooking my left hand on my wheelchair for leverage, I leaned forward to push and twist on the doorknob with my right. The knob got sticky and started to move; Cindy was ready to pounce on the door when she felt it unlatch.

It clicked. I was free! But there was a much bigger click that happened that night, the one in my head. And all hell was about to break loose.

By now, I'd accepted I was handicapped, but I was just starting to realize that I was disabled and what that meant: the physical and mental meld had begun. Why wasn't there a levered handle on that door? I wondered.

Hallelujah, Hooper, you began to see the light. Just breathe. I was crowning, old boy! Hang on.

Then, like a flood, the questions rushed inside my head: How much could it cost to have levered handles on those doors?

Why was "the handicapped parking" area in such a high-traffic danger zone, with cars everywhere?

Why do we have to go in the back door of the school and use The Tunnel to get inside?

Why were all these administrators given parking spots on level ground while the two "handicapped" parking spaces were on a dangerous hill?

Why wasn't there one single parking space with the international wheelchair symbol on it to denote accessible parking for any disabled person, student or not?

Why weren't the rest rooms accessible? (Once I'd had to ask a teacher to empty a leg bag for me before either it or I burst).

Why couldn't we get a drink of water without asking someone for help?

Hey, Hooper, you said WE, not ME. You've almost made it through to the other side. Keep breathing and push.

The system is like The Tunnel. People with disabilities get pigeon-holed and we are told what to accept, what to do, and how to act. We buy into that because we carry the same set of misconceptions about ourselves that able-bodied people have. We accepted our catacomb mode of travel in The Tunnel because for the school it worked. What's that saying: Oppression is most effective when those being oppressed don't know it? In this case, the school probably had no clue they were denying us anything. Like in society itself we were hidden from view because we used the back door. We all thought that this is how it works, and we *all* thought that that was ok. It wasn't ok.

But why should the school change? This works perfect, they thought. As you'll soon find out, they believed they were helping "the handicapped." But they weren't. They were hurting us in such a fundamental way by putting us below everyone else both literally and figuratively. The Tunnel was a symbol of perceived inferiority. We were being forced to accept second-class access every single day because of our disabilities. Eleanor Roosevelt famously said, "*No one can make you feel inferior without your consent.*"

Now you're cooking, Hoop. You guys were like the white rats: you were running the maze, conditioned by your environment and repetitive actions to accept the system without question. Difference is: YOU CAN THINK!

Right, Spokes. This combination of inaccessibility at the school, The Tunnel, our own conditioned attitudes, and the college's "what's-wrong, no-one's-complaining" attitude kept us out of the school's mainstream.

You were locked out by your own free will, Hoop, the perfect oppression. Worked for them, sucked for you.

I know, Spokes. With the click of that door, my mind clicked opened to the realization that there was nothing wrong with any of us. It was *the school. They* were wrong!

Instead of the "hi " and "goodbye'" treatment I had been giving my disabled schoolmates, I started to talk to them about this shitty access we'd been given. There was plenty of agreement, but no action. No one wanted to cause trouble, especially for themselves.

I told the maintenance administrator about having been locked in the building. I requested levered door handles be installed and properly marked parking spaces be made available. He seemed to be in total agreement with my complaints and proposed solutions. But nothing was done.

Next, I drafted a letter (after checking state laws) to both our college and local newspapers telling all: all I knew, anyway. Before I mailed it, I showed my letter to the head of the English Department. He called the Dean of Students.

The Dean read my letter and called me in. I went to see him immediately. "I don't think it would be in your best interests to send this letter," the Dean said in a condescending tone.

"How's that?" I asked, half wondering and half worrying how my protest would affect me at the school.

"We do a lot for the handicapped and are planning to do more," the Dean replied.

"Do you?" I countered. "But is the building in compliance with the law?

"You must know," I continued, "that there's a law requiring state-funded buildings to be accessible to handicapped students. The law is four years old." (I didn't know Section 504 of the US Rehabilitation Act of 1973 even existed, which made the college nine years delinquent in some of its access obligations).

"Yes," the Dean replied, "but this building is not easily made accessible in all areas. We've done our best."

"Really?! Dean. How is it then I can't even get a levered handle on the access door? How is it I got locked in this place? Why can't we get good, safe parking? Why aren't the proper number of parking spaces available and marked? Why is the only thing accessible in this building the telephone?"

The Dean then recited a long list of bullshit, which included irrelevant information about other inaccessible colleges he knew about. The handicapped had always been treated fairly in this college, he maintained. "Why, I even show new handicapped students around our building personally," he boasted.

"You never showed me around the school," I shot back.

"If you send this letter, Ed, you'll not only discredit yourself but our school," he began again, taking another tack. "It's your choice."

Were you getting pissed off yet, Hoop?

Yeah, this attempt at intimidation ticked me off.

I pressed on. "Dean, I've dealt with men like you before. I know lip service when I hear it. I'd like you to respond to these issues by week's end, or I'm sending the letter."

"That would be a mistake, Ed."

"Are you going to get back to me on these things?" I asked.

He said he'd try. He never got back to me, so I sent my letter.

I didn't know about Section 504 and there was no Americans with Disabilities Act (ADA) yet, or much of a disability rights movement for that matter. My letter was full of the wrong language.

What my first letter of protest did have, though, was the seed from which a realization grows; it had the anger that comes from being discriminated against, and *knowing* it. Why had it taken me three to four years to realize I didn't lose my rights because of my disability?

Privately, faculty members and other students were congratulating me for standing up for my rights; but in the public forum, I got only one letter of support from an anonymous student.

We were told that an engineering company was looking into how to make this school as accessible as possible. All was going to be well.

Six months passed, but nothing of substance was started. A letter appeared in the local newspaper by another frustrated disabled student. I wrote another letter to the editor in support and accused the administrators of dragging their feet. Written more than four years after my injury, this letter still showed my ignorance. I wrote to gain sympathy rather than to explain the issues.

It worked; but it was a big mistake. I should have gotten advice. I'd heard of groups in Chicago I could have gotten help from, but I had to be the Disabled Lone Ranger and fight for what I thought was right all by myself.

What's that make me, Tonto? But, hey, it looks like it made a difference.

It did make a difference. The letters, mine and the other man's, prompted a meeting of disabled students, parents and administrators at the school. Because I was no longer a student, I wasn't invited. I went anyway.

The Dean of Students, who was not my number-one fan, took exception to my recommendation that the parking area for disabled students be put closer to the building, in the pick-up circle rather than in the high-traffic area they were now in.

"What are we supposed to do?" he jeered. "Run behind every wheelchair and put a reflector on a stick down your back so you're not hit by traffic?"

Then suddenly out of the depths of my anger, Spokes said through me, "How would you like a reflector stuck up your ass!"

AND SPOKES ABLEMAN WAS BORN!

The president of the school gave the Dean a shut-your-big-mouth look, and the meeting continued.

And, Captain Eddie, we started walking the wheelchair walk.

They finally decided on making a new parking lot, slightly farther from the school than the old parking area, but on level ground. We got an accessible entrance with automatic doors at the front of the building. Special automatic doors, though, that wouldn't open for just anyone. Each disabled student had to carry a garage-door opener to open the doors automatically.

Why? I asked them. Why not just have automatic doors?

Students, I was told. Nondisabled students would screw around with the doors and break them.

Good grief, Hooper. Where do they come up with this shit? To think of 18-and-20-year-old college students jumping up and down on an automatic door pad like 6-year-olds at the grocery store is ludicrous!

I know, right? Besides, grocery stores had survived thirty years of automatic doors use. Stores today have them not for the "handicapped," but because they have proved to be functional, durable, and most helpful to *all* customers.

Unlike those administrators, Hoop, who were neither functional nor helpful. I wonder how the black or female students would have responded to a separate, garage-door-opener entrance for them. Can you visualize that protest?

Yet we still to this day hear these shallow arguments that only serve to segregate us from society, especially when those attitudinal doors are slammed in our faces.

That's true, Hooper. But speaking up makes a difference. We know we can't win them all, maybe not more than 10 or 20%, but it happens bit by bit, not in one big bite.

I know, but I, along with the other disabled students, bought the whole deal. What really happened was that more rest rooms were accessible; water fountains and most elevators were accessible. But much was left inaccessible: the music room, the auditorium, the ramp that must still be there scaring the crap out of people.

Know what else happened, Hoop? Every disabled student from then to now goes in and out the front door of that college, and parks safely. And over these years that you and I have been together, thousands of others like us have fought the fights that opened countless doors for people with disabilities.

This was a win, Hooper. I'd say your first one in a while. Smile!

Happy Birthday Spokes!

CHAPTER 7

HOME SCHOOLING

Ok, Hooper, it's 2015. Does any of this have value in the age of microchips, iPhones, and a black president?

It does, Spokes, it's how I got here and the barriers and challenges I encountered along the way. Attitude-wise, it's not much different now—sometimes it's worse. There are more of us out there because the actual world is more accessible, but sometimes I just throw up my hands and say, there's no way people will ever get this.

Well, Hoop, whodda thunk it? Granpappy Fast Eddie. Your girls, Stacey and Shani, have kids of their own. Alex 6 and James 15. Tick tock.

Spokes, it begins and ends with my three girls: Bunny, Stacey and Shani, and my grandsons. I call the girls my pearls; they shine. And you know the best part?

No, what, old-timer?

It's when your kids grow up. It's cool because they turn into your friends. That's the best. Stacey is a highly respected architect out in Los Angeles. Shani owns her own advertising company. And, well, Cindy, the phrases "through thick and thin" and "for better or worse" are not nearly enough to de-scribe her.

So, Hoops, once I got on the scene back in college everything was jake, right?

Jake? Ableman, are you kidding me with that?

What? Spokes snapped.

No, Spokes, everything was not, as you say, *jake*. I had so very much to learn about living my life with a disability. You don't yank out thirty-two years of negativity like a bad tooth. It was a process, always will be. It's the journey; not the destination.

Thank you, Confucius.

Emerson.

Whatever, Hoop. Fact is you didn't handle things very well during the early years. I call it Disability 101. You were doing D-work with your girls back then, remember?

Yeah, I remember…

"Who was driving?" I asked Stacey disapprovingly.

"Carolyn."

"For Crissake, Stace! You're out drinking 'n driving at 16. Do you wanna be dead?"

"I wasn't driving," Stacey answered.

"Don't be a smart-ass, Stace. You were out in a goddamn car with someone who was drinking."

"Everyone does it, Dad."

"Really. Everyone? Everyone? Everyone? Do you want to end up in a wheelchair the rest of your life? Is that what you want? Huh? Huh? Answer me, goddamnit!"

"No," she replied, cautiously.

I sat there astounded at what happened. I couldn't believe I had actually said from the seat of my wheelchair, "end up in a wheelchair the rest of your life." What was I teaching my girl?

This was the first and last time I used the threat of a wheelchair. But more— too many more—subtle and not-so-subtle scenarios continued to be played out, with different words and different situations, between my two daughters and me. Each negative encounter had essentially the same message: disability was a sharp guilt tool I was capable of wielding with credibility and hurtful effectiveness.

I couldn't admit—or didn't admit—what I was doing.

Well, not until my other daughter, Shani, finally got through to me one day after school:

"Hi, Dad, I'm home."

"Hi, Hon. What'd you do today?" I asked.

"Oh, nothin'. We did some stuff in gym. We had to do these squat-kinda things; they're really hard. Wanna see?"

"No. But you'll probably show me anyway," I said, only half kidding.

"Well, ya get down like this…, and have to bend your legs and do these jump-like things, ya know? I could do the most in my class," she bragged.

"I used to be able to do a hundred of those. You're not doing 'em right, though," I insisted.

"I am, too! It's how our teacher showed us."

"No, you're not. You don't have your hands behind your neck. That makes it a lot harder. That's not how to do 'em," I snorted.

"Better than you can do," she came back defensively.

"Thanks. Thanks a lot," I whined.

"Oh, Dad, you know what I mean."

"Yeah, sure. You know I can't do 'em so... Thanks. Thanks a lot." My voice tailing off, like that of a betrayed friend.

"That's not what I meant!" She insisted.

"Sure," I said, playing the asshole right to the end. Except this time Shani had had enough.

"Dad, you're just doing this to make me feel bad. I wish you'd stop doin' that."

Oh my God! She was right. The words marched through my brain like troops going to war. With five words, my army of guilt slingers were exposed like the shallow little bastards they were: "to make me feel bad. "to make me feel bad." "to make me feel bad." Hut two-three-four.

Yes, I was using my disability to make my daughters feel bad. I was also making me feel bad—really bad.

It became painfully clear: I was unable to face up to myself. My children had always accepted me with and without a disability. It was my prejudice, not theirs. It was my wrongheaded conditioning, not theirs. It was my crippled image, not theirs.

I was teaching them, with extreme negativity, that this "disability pride" thing I was writing and clamoring about was a crock of shit, nothing I actually felt. I was teaching them, through my actions, that guilt should be the product of their forthright interaction with a person with a disability.

Man, this was deep, I thought. Plus I was so envious of my previous physical self. It was frustrating. I got tired of struggling to tell them how I used to do things like hit a softball; I wanted to show them. How does one say he can hit a ball, do a push-up, run a mile, make a basket, climb a hill? When telling my "I-used-to" stories, I felt like a fisherman telling tales of "the-one-that-got-away." It felt empty. All I had, I thought, were empty words. I had something to prove—something I could find no way to prove.

But my words to them were not empty; they were full to the top. Good and bad. The good words were more than enough for my daughters. They accepted me. The bad words were just that, bad words that hurt.

Christ, Hooper, I forgot how messed up that was. My birth obviously didn't flick any switches in your head.

Not at home, not right away, Spokes.

I was using my disability as a weapon. I've always found it difficult to get angry with myself, so my family caught the brunt. They were there all the time; so they saw the dark side. I was pissed. I lost my physical advantage. When the dark emotions grabbed me, I hated being disabled. Despised it! So I'd sometimes snarl, threaten, and sling guilt through the spokes of my wheelchair at my precious girls. It was destructive for all of us.

You know, Hooper, this disability shit isn't like learning how to ride a bike or play guitar. This is hardcore, deep in the brain stuff. You don't suddenly say, 'Hey, this is all cool, and so am I.' It takes time, man.

It sure as hell took me a long time, Spokes. I'd told Stacey and Shani when they were young that they could discuss anything with me: anything. It took a while, but I was finally told what we all knew: My behavior was making everyone, *everyone* "feel bad."

Hopefully, you turned this around quickly, Fast Eddie.

Well, Spokes, there's one more eye-opening story.

Oh, no, Hooper not more exposure to mean-self-centered-Hooper.

Nah, Spokes, this was downright insightful. While I was taking psychology (no wise cracks Ableman), we were talking about persona and how we often show different people different faces. I knew this to be true, but I was curious to know how my friends perceived me post-injury. Was I different besides the obvious physical change?

I decided to include my oldest daughter Stacey in the little mini-study. Shani was still a bit young to do it, I thought. I made out a questionnaire and let six or seven friends and Stacey fill it out. It was one of those 1 to 10 type things where 1 was lowest and 10 the highest. I was utterly shocked at the contrast between my friends' answers and Stacey's:

Friends: funny – Stacey: humorless
Friends: outgoing – Stacey: closed off
Friends: happy – Stacey: dour

It went on and on, Spokes, with almost every question receiving an almost opposite answer from Stacey to that of my friends.

Oh, Hoop, that is seriously fucked up. That's worse than mean-self-centered Hooper.

I know, Spokes. I wasn't being my true self to my own family. But, man, that opened my eyes, and I set out to change my ways, not overnight mind you, but I knew what to do and started doing it. First, I apologized.

Oh, yeah, you were going through the steps of DA.

DA, Ableman?

Disability Anonymous.

Are you kidding me, Spokes?

No, Hoop, but there's really only one step.

Yeah, and what's that?

Admit in your heart and mind that you have a disability, Hooper.

Stacey and Shani

My daughters and wife have taught me well. It's been well over 30 years since I apologized for my guilt-slinging behavior. And somehow over the years I lost most of my anger, pre-disability anger as well. It melted away through hard work and through the positive influence of my pearls, my girls.

Three Pearls

It is an honor being loved by you
You give richness and luster to my life
May that love somehow outlive the earth and the stars

To shine with a light of its own
And give always what I've had from the start
My girls
My pearls
The pearls of my heart

My mother used to tell me, "You seem to learn only one way: the hard way." Like many things my mother said, that too is true.

• • •

My three pearls and I took a cross-country trip in the early eighties, cruising out to California to see friends, the sites, and to go to Disneyland in the War Wagon. The War Wagon was my first accessible vehicle, a black Dodge van with a white topper. It was equipped with a wheelchair lift to get me in, and hand controls so I could drive it.

The Hoopers were the first Griswolds, headed out to our Wally World, and also looking for a new place to live—somewhere warm. This was the best vacation I ever took in my life, and it would have been even better if I hadn't still been carrying a lot of injury baggage along with me as described earlier in this Chapter. But the girls didn't care; they had just gotten out of school for the summer and we were on the road. It was four great weeks.

Want to make Stacey and Shani smile? Two words: Cline's Corner. We did a ton of great family stuff on this trip from the Meramec Caverns in Missouri to the Grand Canyon to San Diego to L.A. to San Francisco to Reno back to the Midwest. We even saw the end of a rainbow in Nebraska—seriously, we did. But none of all those stops and countless other places along the way were more memorable in our hearts, minds, and noses than the gas and tourist stop called Cline's Corner in New Mexico.

We were in our third day on the road and the weather had been perfect, no rain and in the 70s. My system was not used to travel and road-food, but I was doing really well. No problems, not until Cline's Corner, that is. There is no good way to write about this.

What, you crapping your pants at an inaccessible tourist stop in the middle of New Mexico?

All right, Ableman, shut up.

Why? It happens, Fast Eddie. In this case, faster than you thought.

Very funny, Spokes, and it does suck in the biggest of ways. But come on!

You'll have to admit, Hoop, that wheelchair users will never master the skill of getting to and getting on the pot in a timely manner.

Well, that's for sure.

So accidents do happen.

But do you we have to talk about it?

Yeah, we do. Not dwell, but acknowledge. For me, anyway, with all my high-winded touting of the disability experience, this is something I'll never be totally good with.

Me either, Spokes.

Why should we have to, Hooper? It happens. Tell your story.

There we all were with the nearest accessible restroom 50 miles away, and the van starting to, well, stink—really stink. Worse, I was the source. The kids jumped out like a couple of crickets, and sat patiently on the curb while I got onto the fold-down back seat and we (meaning Cindy) cleaned up the mess. Shitty work. The kids shuttled soap and water, and they were actually far better at dealing with the whole ordeal than me. I was embarrassed and pissed off at the same time, which can make for explosive behavior. Stacey and Shani smartly stayed out of any possible blast zone. But I managed to suck it up without going ballistic. An hour for clean-up and two extra strength Imodium Ads later, we were on our way fresh and clean. Happily, there were no more Cline's Corners incidents the rest of the trip.

Why do I mention this with all the TMI implications, and why do we laugh about it to this day? First, laughter is liberating. Second, the mere mention of Cline's Corner instantly captures a shared experience as valid to our family trip as Disneyland or Universal Studios or Fisherman's Wharf or anywhere else we went. No, it's more valid. It makes us all smile and say, "Oh my God, Cline's Corner." Enough said. It doesn't have to be happy, squeaky clean to be an "it doesn't get any more real than that" story. Cline's Corner has morphed its way into a fond, funny family memory because it's about us together, on the road—our family enjoying the gift of one another's company even in the stinkiest of times.

Fast forward. Thirty years after Cline's Corner, I'm driving back from Winter Haven, Florida with Stacey, Cindy, and my 4½-year-old grandson Alex in one car. Jim and Shani were in her car. The whole family went up to Legoland for the day. It was a long, hot, hot day. Ironically, Legoland is built on one giant mass of solid concrete and it was hell-hot. Alex loved it.

We made it through the day, and were heading home on I-75, when just kidding I said to Bunny, "Watch the wheel in case I fall asleep." What happened next I have not been able to accurately recreate because neither I nor Stacey nor Cindy can remember the barrage of questions that came my way, nor can I capture the tone and syntax Alex used. We all agree that what took place next was both intensely serious and incredibly thorough. Yet Stacey and Cindy had to bite their lips from laughing.

Alex had become increasingly curious about my injury and disability. Up to then, that curiosity was quickly dealt with by just saying that I was injured in a car accident and that I couldn't walk anymore. Not this day. My "sleep" comment channeled Alex's inner cross-examining attorney because he promptly asked, "What you said"? That's how he asks, "What did you say"?

"I was just kidding," I quickly pointed out.

"Pop, how did you get in your accident"? He immediately shot back.

"Well, I fell asleep and ran off the road."

"Why, were you tired?"

"Yes."

"Were you going fast?"

"Yes."

"Really fast?"

"Yeah, kinda like we are now," I answered.

"Where did you go off the road?"

"Into an area in the middle like over there," I explained while pointing at the median strip.

"What happened?"

"Well, I hit a ditch," I replied

"How?"

"The car ran into it," I told him

"Then what happened?" He promptly asked.

"The car flipped over."

"And you were hurt?"

"Yes, Big Boy, my neck was broken."

"And you couldn't walk after that?"

"No."

"Why?"

"Well, I was injured," I answered.

"Didn't you go to the doctor?"

"Yes, I did."

"Didn't he fix your boo-boo?"

"No."

"Why?"

"It just something that couldn't be fixed," I responded, starting to feel a little like the guy being interrogated with a hot light in his face.

There were a good fifteen minutes of questions. So many that I can't really recall them all except that there was no wiggle room for bullshit. Alex's line of questioning wasn't about to let me squirm my way out, and I was about ready to break down yell, "Yes, yes, I did it! I did it! I was drinking and driving and broke my neck!" I didn't say that, of course. I just answered the questions as honestly and concisely as possible.

When it was over, Alex then gave his summation: "Pop, you were driving and fell asleep and crashed the car and couldn't walk no more, right?"

"Yes, that's right," I replied.

"You're not going to fall asleep now are you, Pop?"

"No, Big Boy, I'm not. Don't worry."

We all quickly realized that he was as interested in not having a repeat performance with all of us in the car as he was in my injury and accident. Stacey, Bunny and I were sorry Jim and Shani weren't with us to witness the young Perry Mason at work. Me? I was just happy the questioning had stopped.

Christmas

Our family has no blanket rules, save one: Obey the Sisterhood (Bunny, Stacey, Shani) and you'll be fine. Unlike a popular theme that appears in books and movies, there are never any blow-ups at our family gatherings where a crazy uncle goes on an insane rant, ending with him throwing the turkey carcass across the room at a parent or sibling. But we do tend to laugh a lot. We don't meddle, we advise. We don't belittle, we encourage. We love one another at the deepest levels. We have kind, thoughtful, honest, and dependable kids, and, of course, wonderful grandkids. In short, Cindy and I are blessed.

I do have one mandatory obligation: No matter what, the family must be together at Christmas. It is our ritual; it is sacred to me, and to them too, I think, although they might not use that word. We see each other far more often than once a year, but Christmas is a must-do. Now, Stacey, Paul, and Alex live in Burbank, CA so that trip can get costly, but between us we always find a way. Shani and Jim live in Sarasota.

Our ritual really begins on Christmas Eve. Without putting a name on it or making a big deal out of it, we gather together for both ourselves and for those who have gone before us.

Bunny makes BBQ pork or beef in honor of her father Iggy. He was part of what has been called the "greatest generation." He fought three-plus years in WW-II in the Pacific—he was awarded the Purple Heart and a chest full of other medals. He came home and started a family and worked every day for 35 years at a cement factory from 6 a.m. to 3 p.m., sometimes nights. Iggy and his wife Gertrude raised four children that each grew up to be valuable additions to this society. He was self-educated and smart, very smart. Our tribute to Iggy comes in the form of his tradition of making BBQ every Christmas Eve. We would all go to his house early in the evening, and as soon as you walked in from the cold Illinois winter, you could smell the BBQ simmering on the stove that he had prepared and pulled earlier. And before church (he and I never went), we all had a BBQ or two with assorted other goodies like cheese, chips, potato salad, olives, potica (Slovenian cakes made by Gert), etc. Some of us would have a beer or four. Cindy, her mom, her sister and the kids would then go off to church while two or three of us pagans hung out and bullshitted until they all got back home, and then we would open gifts.

So, our Christmas ritual starts out very much the same: the BBQ is simmering. Stacey, Paul, and Alex are already here, as they arrive a day or two early and they stay with us. Shani and Jim and now Eddie (Shani's longtime boyfriend and fiancé as of New Year's Eve) arrive around 5 p.m. The eating starts in earnest almost immediately, but the similarities to the days of yore stop right there. First, I don't (can't!) drink beer anymore. My stomach rebels in a most vile manner. Second, we all go to church after eating.

I cannot go into why I go to church now and not then, because I'm not 100 percent sure myself why. Back then, it was something about growing up Catholic and no longer believing in God. I now joke that I'm cramming for finals. Suffice to say that church feels right, words I never thought I'd utter. I've never been particularly religious, but I've always been spiritual, and I've always loved "Silent Night," which might be the most beautiful song ever written. Before my injury, I learned to play "Silent Night" on guitar, a version that moved up and down the whole neck of the guitar. I practiced my ass off and it sounded pretty good. Ironically, I would play it at Iggy's house when the others were off at church singing, among other things, "Silent Night."

St. Andrew, the church we belong to now, stresses spirituality over dogma. Sometimes the inside of St. Andrew feels like a "thin place." The Celtics call a "thin place" a place that gets one closer to what we cannot understand, a closeness to our essence perhaps. That place cannot be searched for, but it can be experienced by both one's presence and receptiveness. This is especially true with the Christmas Eve service at St. Andrew. Once—with music that included the magical "Holy Night," and ended with a beautiful candlelight singing of "Silent Night"—a "thin place" opened and I felt a fierce peace that got me closer to something far beyond me. God? I don't know, probably not. But it was a powerful peace that played inside of me until "sleep in heavenly peace" was sung and we raised the candles high for just a moment or two before blowing them out and heading into the night.

So, we all go to church, which is the start of the Santa Claus show. First it was for Jim, and now it's for Alex who probably has one or two more Santa encounters left before some little creep at school blows the whistle on the whole wonderful deception. As we pile into the cars to go to church, we have two people lag behind to pull out all the gifts and put them under the tree. Alex has already left milk and a cookie, so they take a bite, careful to leave crumbs, and take a big drink of milk. On the way home, we talk up the whole Santa visit story. As we drive up to the house someone shouts, "Oh my gosh, what was that flash in the sky...we just missed him!" Alex races into the house where he finds an avalanche of presents under the tree waiting for him, and then we must somehow divert his enthusiasm until we can all get inside and settled; he cannot be deterred for long.

But first we must take the family photo. Each year turns into a "how-to" on using the camera's self-timer because we forget how the settings work from the previous year. So, with Alex about ready to go bonkers, we figure that out and all get in front of the tree. Bunny sets up the camera and pushes the button and races over to take her spot. Three, two, one and "click" we get the shot, but there's always some issue with smiles or poses or position or light. With Alex ready to do some serious ripping of the wrapping paper, we say, "Come on, just one more." And like a trooper he and we do it again, and again. By the time it's over we're all ready to get the show on the road.

**Last Christmas: L-R Paul, Stacey, Bunny,
Shani, Jim, Eddie. Front: Alex, Me**

The next act is the opening of gifts.

No way, Hoop. Too many presents! An avalanche?

What, are you some kind of Grinch, Ableman?

No, Eddie Who, I'm fed up with things, things, things, shop-ping, shopping, shopping and not giving, giving, giving, which is the whole point. Why, I remember us getting practically nothing. Some years mom couldn't even afford heat for the house, but we always had each other as we huddled around the tree.

That is precisely the point, Spokes. We gather in the living room and start opening gifts, but what we're really opening is our hearts to one another. It's a ritual in that we take turns opening gifts, and we usually have a comment or two about how nice the earrings are or how great the shirt is, or, "Where did you get that?" Or, "Remember that time we…". Story after story. Each year, after all the gifts are opened, I go to where I've hid the presents I had gotten for my Three Pearls. Everybody knows I'm going to do it, but they pretend they don't notice me slip away to get the gifts, which I hide in the same place every year—they all know that too. But it's not the gifts I'm giv-ing. It's not the physical gifts any of us are giving. Our gifts are usually thoughtful and nice, never expensive, but it's the love that comes with the giving and receiving that puts the music to our Christmas Eve waltz. That love too can be a "thin place," and I tear-up just talking about it.

I still think it's too much, Hooper.

It is, Spokes, but live with it.

I do. I actually love it in spite of myself.

The next day Cindy's brother Terry, his wife Joan, and their son Erik come over to join us all for Christmas Dinner. Terry brings a huge, yummy ham he prepares with pineapple circles, cloves, and glazing. Joan usually brings a dessert, and Cindy fixes the other fixings, including her award-winning scallop potatoes. Yum! We put on some holiday music, banter back and forth, talk about those old days, tell a few lies, eat like little pigs, and lay around afterward groaning about how tired and full we are.

Christmas Day always makes me think about my mother, too, because before mom's death in 1979, Cindy and I and the kids all went to her house for Christmas dinner. Mom's name was Jean. She always had a plump turkey with mashed potatoes, great stuffing, pumpkin pie, and all the rest. She was a good cook, especially at Christmas.

My mother had a tough go of it in life, though, tougher than most. My father who was the love of mom's life died when she was 29. Like Iggy, my dad was also wounded and decorated in WW-II. He was in Africa and Europe. Two months before his untimely death in 1954, due to a systemic infection that spread from a cut fin-

1-year-old Fred & Mom

ger (a freaking finger!), my mother gave birth to Cathy who was born with Down Syndrome. In those days people with Down Syndrome were called Mongoloids, and the stigma piled onto my mother and sister was palpable around our small town: You and yours are majorly flawed.

My brother Fred, named for my father, was 12 and he never fully recovered from the trauma of our dad's death. It crushed him. I was 8 years and 2 months old, yet try as I may, I don't have *one single* memory of my dad—*not one*. He was there everyday, played ball with us, took us to movies, fishing, grandma's house, you name it, but I can't remember anything of him. Don was only 2 years old; he has no memories of any of it.

What I do remember, like a dark, distant echo, is my mom wailing and sobbing uncontrollably, the grief filling the house thick with pain—no words exist for that, only tears. She sank to the bottom of her soul and never fully recovered. I have no idea how long it went on, weeks, months, but it exposed my helplessness and inability to understand. I'd ask, "Ma, are you ok?" She'd usually say, "It's ok, mommy doesn't feel well." I'm sure my father's death and my mother's suffering wounded me greatly, but I have no clue how badly.

Here is a current conversational memory of Christmas in 1955, the year after my father's death:

Well, Hoop, Thursday is Christmas.

Yep, Spokes, love Christmas—especially Christmas Eve!

Not too commercial for you, Hoop?

Heck, no. The holidays are a time to kick the dust off the wallets and spend a few bucks on loved ones and those in need.

You don't think it goes too far?

Of course, Spokes, we always go too far. This is America.

What are your best Christmas memories, Hooper.

God, I have so many. Our family is quite close, especially around this time of year. It would take till New Years 2020 to cover them all.

But to go back into my childhood, it's my mother.

You had a mom, Hooper?

Ha, Ha. Very funny, Ableman.

Sorry, Hoop. Besides the obvious, why was she special?

As you know, we were poor growing up. So were a lot of my friends, but I never knew who was poor and who wasn't. Some kids had Papermate pens, nice clothes, and shoes without holes in the soles, but somehow at 8 or 9 years old, I didn't think about that as rich or poor. That's just how it was.

Yeah, Hoop, I don't remember any prejudice from that time in my life, except I know that no one liked the Japanese and Germans—they were mostly called Japs and Krauts.

Anyway, Spokes, I think I still believed in Santa Claus. The year after my father died, it didn't look like Christmas was coming for us. I was nine. It was December in Illinois, and we ran out of heating oil. That happened every once in a while at the end of the month. We'd turn on the gas stove, open up the oven door, and gather around trying to warm up.

God, I hate being cold, Hooper.

Me too, Spokes.

We always had a tree though, Hoop, with those hot bulbs that would burn the crap out of you if you even touched them.

Yeah, they burned down many-a house, too. No fires at our house, though.

Thank God for small favors is what Ma used to say.

This year things were really lean, as I said. My mother was preparing us for a slim Christmas, saying things like, 'Santa is very busy this year.' I think she wanted us believing in Santa as long as possible. We never expected much anyway, but that didn't make the whole experience any less exciting.

My aunt, who bought us socks every year when we really could have used shoes, must have called the Salvation Army because they showed up at our house with presents.

Remember what Ma said about that, Hoop?

Nothing to us, but she must have said plenty to her sister because the good folks at the Salvation Army never came back. I think my mom was embarrassed and ticked.

She kicked some sister-ass after that, I'm sure, and the financial need lessened as the years passed. But not this year.

Yeah, Spokes, this was the low point in our money situation; things got better little by little, year by year. When I was 15 my mother remarried.

I forgot, what did the Salvation Army bring?

I can't remember what my brothers Fred and Don got, and my sister, Cathy, was still a baby, but I got a cap gun, a cowboy cap gun. It had those caps that popped when you pulled the trigger.

That's pretty cool, Hooper.

Not really, Spokes, the gun was broke. The trigger didn't work so it was a point-and-say-bang-bang gun, which worked for us. Heck, we could make a gun out of just about anything anyway, so it worked as good as a stick.

Hell, I always had my finger fully loaded and ready to fire. What else did you get?

Toy-wise, nothing. At that time, my mother worked as a waitress at a place called The Ranch House. She was a single mom who worked for tips to raise four kids. My sister was just over a year old, and Down Syndrome at that time was looked at as a curse and stigma to both her and her parents.

So, what else did we get? We got my mom and evidently she got us. She filled us with warmth and love at a time of great hardship.

She was there. I can smell her now, Spokes. She would gather us around and she was like a warm fire no matter how cold it was. I don't remember any words of wisdom, or any miracles of Christmas that filled the heating oil tanks or our stockings, or any magic that created trains and toys under the tree. What I do remember is the sheer presence of my mother.

And the next day we'd go to my grandma's house and have turkey.

When December 26th came, Ma would be back to waiting tables.

But on Christmas Eve, it was just us, sitting around the warm fire of my mother's love. She was able to give this gift in spite of everything she had to face. That is love and courage.

Turns out, Spokes, for me and my brothers and sister, the gift of love was more than enough. And in spite of my sarcastic nature, I try to pass it on.

"Merry Christmas, Spokes."

Merry Christmas, Hoop.

Jean went on to raise four kids by working her ass off as a waitress for seven years until she married Andy, my stepfather. But during those years like Christmas 1955, we had each other, as does my family now. Obviously, we're now much better off financially, but the spiritual message is the same: be together. My mom—and by all accounts my dad—would be most proud of our Christmas ritual and of us.

So as a family, we celebrate our roots and ourselves in both thick and thin places. We remember and we make new memories. The chorus to my song "Hold On" says some of it:

> Hang on to your memories
> They might be the only things
> That ever keep you sane
> Hold on tight
> And always know
> It's the only way that I can be
> Wherever you will go.

You're still learning, Little Eddie Who.

I know, Spokes, because I've got some really good teachers.

CHAPTER 8

SEXUALITY (IT DOES WORK)

"No, I guess I have always felt that you are paralyzed, and you have no sexual life. And, you know, that is just part of it. That's part of being disabled. Ahhh, umm, I don't think you have gotten less masculine because of it or anything; it, I think, is just something that doesn't work."

This quote, coming from one of my best friends, set me back on my wheely-bars. Bob has helped me in more ways since my injury than any friend I can think of. He has a college education, and he's successful in business. Bob's words came in response to one of ten broad-reaching questions I'd asked several friends regarding my disability in general and how they perceived it. The question: Do you wonder about my sexuality, like what feeling I have, excitement, etc.?

Everyone else I'd asked sidestepped the question by saying that it was a private matter, and that they wouldn't want me to know about their sex lives. I do understand and respect their reticence, because serious discussion about sexuality must be the most inhibiting topic in our culture. But what, I thought —within contemporary sexual behavior—could these people have experienced sexually that I didn't know about? I've been in their position; they've not been in mine. They were curious, I'd concluded, but the question was too intimidating.

Not Bob, though. I'd asked him to be honest, and he laid it out in his uncanny style: "It... just... doesn't work." Although I was upset that such a close friend thought, for so many years, that my disability meant I was sexually inactive, I was sure the majority of society held the same opinion. Listeners had little trouble believing that old Kenny Rogers song, "Ruby," wherein her husband, a paralyzed Vietnam veteran pleads with Ruby not to "take" her "love to town." The lyrics are so brutally cruel to every person who sits in a wheelchair that I can hardly type them. Yet that's what the writer, singer, and listeners believe as being true—matter-of-factly slapping us down while probably not even realizing it.

The movie *Murderball* takes a bite out of that stereotype. But with the notable exception of the film, *Coming Home*, where a paralyzed veteran is depicted as a vital, sexual individual, the visual media have perpetuated the myth, even to the point of a paralyzed man, in the asinine TV movie *Thou Shalt Not Commit Adultery*, giving permission for a surrogate to screw his wife. My God! The thought of such a sick-premised movie makes my moral skin crawl. To think viewers find it more plausible for a man or woman to sit consentingly in their wheelchair outside a bedroom door while some dildo with a human body attached to it is satisfying their spouse/partner is nauseating. But, obviously, it's far more plausible to the writers, the directors, the producers, the actors, and probably the viewers than having the person with the disability inside that bedroom sharing intimate sex with the person they love.

This Lady Chatterley mentality has unjustly neutered us and turned our partners into celibates, or, what's worse, turned them into deprived, depraved, lustful creatures on the prowl. So there are two people being debased in these depictions: if I am perceived as asexual, then my wife must either be a saint to preserve our sexless relationship, or a sinner, like Rogers' "Ruby"—or the countless other distortions—to get satisfied elsewhere.

So here we are again in society's asylum. This time we're scream-ing, "We *have* sexuality! We *have* sexuality!" I can almost hear the consoling whispers, "Of course you do. Of course you do. Shhhhh...."

Well, I wasn't going to let Bob out of my house without telling him it was my neck I'd broken, not my libido. But what and how would I tell him? A person's sexuality, like the individual, is unique. I wasn't going to verbalize some kind of makeshift disability Kama Sutra, nor offer Bob an uninformed peep into someone else's bedroom. I needed to look back to my experience, and from what I'd learned, so I could dis-pel the myths and misconceptions about my general sexuality, which in turn would inform him that people, like me, with paralyzing disabilities are indeed sexual human beings.

The brain is the cornucopia of sexuality. Neurologists call it "the sexiest organ in the body." It sends and receives all the messages from fantasy to arousal, analyzes the bodies' response, and, if all is going well, provides an array of pleasure. Before my injury, for me sexual pleasure was derived primarily from a sensual, erect—or soon to be erect—penis. My dick ruled. After I broke my neck, I became acutely conscious of the brain-penis disconnection: I had little or no feeling in the latter. How, I kept asking myself, could I possibly give, or, what was more difficult to comprehend, attain sexual satisfaction with an insentient penis?

I think we men learn at a young age that masculinity is measured by the erected inch, and then most of us slowly unlearn that absurdity. But erections are important to men; we like our hard-ons. Unlike suf-focation, however, we can live sexually active and happy lives without actually feeling penile arousal or "getting it up" for that matter. When I finally got the nerve to look at my body, I was amazed that with direct stimulation I could get and maintain an erection. (This is not true of everyone, however, but implants and prosthetics are available to those individuals who themselves feel these are necessary to their and their partner's sexual and psychological well-being.)

Still, no feeling, though. But disability can teach us profound lessons in loss and coping, and I know that for me, by using my penis—despite having no pre-injury feeling in it—if I am giving pleasure, then I am also receiving pleasure. That "sexiest organ in the body" can be a most amatory sensor.

My brain was working the day I attended a peer-group seminar on sexuality and disability. I soon found out that they knew how important sex was to disabled individuals. At that time, they were trying to quell the obsession for what they called "The Big 0": Orgasm. It was quite possible, they said, for only one person or neither person to reach an orgasm (at least as we knew it before disability) and still experience totally fulfilling intimacy.

I had my doubts, but it's true. My brain remains unconvinced of my rumored asexuality, and keeps sending erotic messages, but my main focus of sensual reception has changed from my penis to other areas of my body. I have feeling in my extreme upper body: shoulders, upper-chest, parts of my arms, neck, lips, ears, etc., and with intimate contact of these areas, and knowing I'm also giving pleasure by kissing, touching and embracing, my heart begins to race. My head gets warm. My mind surges to give and to get more; and I aggressively pursue those impulses and feelings. My muscles tense-up, and quickly the excitement increases to a level of intense pleasure and then subsides towards contentment.

It's not like ejaculation; the loss of control is less convulsive. It's more like an orgasm, but without the same intensity brought on by ejaculation. The distinction is that orgasm, as I now know it, is the pleasurable conclusion of making love. I have actually ejaculated on occasion, so in no way do I believe the experience is totally a mental phenomenon. My sexual pleasure is more of a physical and mental meld, and when something erotic is happening, I try not to force it, but let both my body and mind respond. I could have used this insight before my disability, because, although I have had many, many beautiful encounters with my wife, too often I'd let my corporal-self deprive me of the immense mental pleasure brought on by love-making. Mentally, sex is now a lot better. Physically, it's now less intense than was my good pre-disability sex, but most fulfilling, nonetheless.

What do my wife and I miss? Well, spontaneity, for one. We must plan our encounters more than we had to before. We sometimes miss my ability to get on top, too. With a little adaptation and creative thinking even those types of bugaboos can be overcome. We miss stand-up sex too, but we occasionally want to take a stroll in the woods, and do other pre-disability activities, as well. I can't do some of those things.

My sexuality is a matter of knowing what my functional capabilities are and fitting those into a mutually satisfying sexual encounter with my wife. Cindy and I both have had to adjust to my disability. We live with it. We love with it.

In Erich Fromm's "The Art of Loving," he writes, "The sexual act without intimacy retains a separateness that cannot be forgotten by orgasm." Fromm's words remind me of Jack Nicholson's character in *Carnal Knowledge*. He had beautiful women and orgasms a sex-crazed Roman would have envied, but he never sought love and ended up as a pitiful, middle-aged lecher paying a prostitute for "dirty words" and blow jobs.

Disabled or nondisabled, we all deserve the opportunity for the closeness, the intimacy, the mutually accepted pleasure of one another as sexual human beings. As Fromm suggests, we need to love and to be loved.

I gathered my thoughts and explained to Bob my sexual vitality. His reaction: "All these years, geez, I can't believe it. That shocks me. I want to go out and tell everyone. I'm sure everyone else thinks the same thing because when you say you are paralyzed from the neck down, you know... I can't believe it. That's out of this whole deal (the interview)—that's what shocks me."

I doubt if Bob told too many people. Based on what we are being fed by literature and the media, no one he told believed him anyway.

Hooper, do you know how hard it was not to say anything during this little erotic lecture of yours? In one spot I was getting a boner.

A boner, Ableman? What are you, 13?

Never mind that. You missed something.

Really, what's that?

Kids. Paralyzed people make babies. Some do it the old-fashioned way, some with artificial insemination or in vitro.

Good point, Spokes. I personally know at least ten spinal cord injured people myself who have had children and are now raising them. And just like able-bodied folks, some have chosen adoption as a means to have a family.

Bottom line, Hoop, gimps can be good parents, too.

Yes they can. Spinal cord injured women can get pregnant and deliver healthy babies?

Google it, old timer. Of course they can.

Sexuality in people with paralyzing disabilities is alive. It must be given a chance to bud and bloom. Yes, we love, we get horny, we communicate, we kiss, we touch, we get jealous, we have emotional pain, and yes, we experience and enjoy sex. And we have families. We mustn't, through ignorance and simple-minded stereotypes, allow ourselves to be labeled sexually dead. I shudder to think of how much love and lovemaking have been abandoned because one or both persons thought, "It just doesn't work."

It does!

CHAPTER 9

THE DISABILITY RAG

Spokes, I remember the first time I saw a copy of the *Disability Rag*—that beat-up little magazine. The copy the guy gave me looked like it was printed on old comic book paper, without the glossy cover. I started reading it out of pure curiosity, and it changed my life. The stories were different, eye-opening stories that looked back at society and said, "It's your perceptions that are the problem here, not ours."

Yeah, Hooper, at first you thought it was a bunch of bullshit.

I did, Spokes. But the more I read this magazine, the clearer it all became. Sure there were physical barriers like curbs, doors, stairs, inaccessible transportation, etc. But the attitudes were and still are the toughest.

Attitude, Hoop, the big one—the iceberg of barriers we talk about.

Yep, it's the iceberg that we have yet to melt. Anyway, the subscription was five bucks. Five bucks! So I sent it in and the *Rag* started to reshape my thinking about living with a disability.

You didn't even think of it that way back then, Hooper. You didn't think 'living with,' you thought that somehow the disability was you. You were a quad. But The Rag said, you are a person first and your disability is just another part of who you are.

Sounds so simple now, Spokes.

That's because it's so incredibly easy to understand, Hoop, but it's hidden in plain sight. Our culture and society is set to believe that the disability is who we are, and it is almost impossible to rethink and understand that without some help.

I know, Spokes. I did a little presentation recently at our church on what they called Access Sunday. I talked about the physical barriers I still encounter—although there are far fewer now than back in the '80s. But my mission was attitudes.

Tell me you didn't use the graveyard photo up on the big screen.

I did.

The one on Facebook that got millions of views and likes and thousands of positive comments?

That's the one.

The one of a gravestone with a statue of an 8 or 9-year-old child set on top ascending into heaven out of the seat of a wheelchair?

Yep.

You did this in a church? Are you nuts? What did you say?

Well, it went like this after the physical barriers portion of the talk:

Attitudinal barriers are locked up far more securely. I'm going to show you something that millions have seen on Facebook recently (a half million likes as of a month ago and with thousands of positive comments). You might also like it and find it inspirational, and emotional, and at some level you might say, "Ah, yes, free at last."

Or, you might be like me.

At first I found this image a bit creeeeepy, but I also happen to find it offensive, and I'll tell you why. I do totally get why one wouldn't want to be in a wheelchair because I'd been in your shoes for 32 years—and 35 on wheels. It took me a while to see myself as myself. And I get the parents' sentiment for a son who may have suffered from any number of things. Who knows what?

But this is so over-the-top through its graveyard theatrics that it sends a negative message via the viral social media about thousands and thousands of us who use wheelchairs, and who are doing quite well, thank you.

You need to know that my chair is not a torture chamber or a prison. I *AM NOT* confined to it. In fact, my actual freedom comes *because* of this wheelchair. I access *this world, this church*, I access you, I access everyone I know and everywhere I go *with* this wheelchair. Without it, well, that might be that other place we hear about with the ragged clothes, dark caves, and flaming hot coals. I wonder what the design on that kind of gravestone might look like. Yikes!

Imagine with me for a few seconds that instead of the wheelchair user a black man was depicted as turning white ascending into heaven, or a woman turning into a man. Absurd, right? But there are still people who believe that Blacks, women, gays, lesbians, Muslims, and countless others can't even get into heaven. *That's* inaccessibility, my friends. You're locked out for eternity. At least—according to this depiction—I can get in. But for me, there's a catch: I have to leave the wheelchair behind for the *full, 100%* heaven experience. Sort of like Disneyworld, I guess.

You read this in church?

Yes, at St. Andrew United Church of Christ in Sarasota.

Damn, Hoop, sorry I missed that. If the Bears weren't playing Washington on that Sunday, I would have definitely been there cheering you on. And how was it received?

Extremely well, Spokes. Although, I'm not quite sure how the actual visual of the gravestone was received and perceived. I have a hunch many may have liked the basic emotion and idea of being free from a wheelchair. I ended the talk with this:

> If there is a heaven and if God sees fit to let me in, I hope it's with the wheelchair—although, heaven's wheelchairs would have to be pretty darn cool looking, right? I'm thinking, very sporty, easy to push, cloud-like model, with a Love In Action logo on both sides. Thank you and God bless.

So the Disability Rag cranked up your engine to this way of thinking."

Sure did. Wanna know the real irony? The editor of the *Rag*, Mary Johnson[9], didn't have a physical disability.

Seriously?

Seriously. She is an able-bodied person who gained her understanding from interaction with people with disabilities in Louisville—initially the concept of inclusion came from her feelings about civil rights and the women's movement. A co-organizer, Cass Irvin, who *does* have a disability, talked the little ragtag group into going national. They decided to publish the *Disability Rag* themselves nationally through the newly-incorporated Advocado Press. Activists around the country took to the *Rag* almost immediately and Disability Rights and Independent Living had a voice.

We heard that voice, Hooper.

Yeah, we sure did, Spokes.

wrote a poem called "The Way Downtown" and sent it to Mary Johnson. She told me that the *Disability Rag* didn't use much poetry, but the poem was about transportation and inclusion, which were (and are!) important issues. To my surprise, she published it, and later published others.

But Johnson wanted more from me. We talked and I told her some of the stories I've told here in *Don't Push Me*. She wanted me to write

9 http://media-dis-n-dat.blogspot.com/2009/04/founder-of-disability-rag-tells-its.html

them. I said, no way; I'm a poet and songwriter, the wannabe variety. She convinced me to try, and, with her expert help in editing, most of my early disability stories appeared in the *Rag*. In fact, for a time we (the Advocado Press and me) regularly submitted disability-related Op-Ed stories to the major newspapers in the US and many of those were published. Sadly, I can't find the tear sheets from papers like *The Cleveland Plain Dealer, Seattle Post-Intelligencer, Rocky Mountain News* (now gone), *The New York Times, Dallas Morning News, Atlanta Constitution, Louisville Courier-Journal*, and others I can't even recall. My Aphasia story from Chapter Four was published in *Mother Jones*. So we had some traction in the mainstream media, limited footing but a start.

I decided to go to Louisville and meet face-to-face with Mary Johnson, Cass Irvin, Mary Jane Owen who is blind, and others.

Oh, boy, Hooper, I stepped in it there, didn't I?

You certainly did, Ableman. It's your nature.

Shit. We're all sitting around talking about this and that when someone brought up the great songs from the musical <u>Cats</u>. Bunny and I had recently seen the show in Chicago and Mary and her husband had seen it as well. We were raving about it. Mary Jane popped into the conversation and said, 'Yes, I bought the CD.' Remember what I said, Hoop?

Vividly, Spokes.

I said, "Well, of course, you would just get the CD."

Mary Jane pounced on me and said, 'Why wouldn't I want to go to the theater to experience the ambience, the character and atmosphere of a play or musical? Why would I JUST get the CD?'

Ouch!

Well, Fast Eddie, I backpedaled like a politician caught with his paw stuffing the ballot box, but it was a pathetic effort. I stammered and stuttered for about 30 seconds (seemed like an hour). But I was exposed in a room full of disability activists for making uninformed judgments about someone's disability. Humiliated, I simply apologized. Jesus, that hit home hard, Hooper.

Sure did, Spokes.

I'd been spouting off in print and in discussions about preconceived ideas people have about disability, and there I was doing the same damn thing. I, of all people, should have known better.

We should have, Spokes, but didn't.

The *Rag* was that conscience we all needed. That inner voice to remind us that this inclusion and independent living stuff we were talking about applied to everyone, not just spinal-cord-injured people or post-polio people or people with Multiple Sclerosis or blind people or deaf people or whatever—it applied to all of us.

The *Rag* first came out in January 1980. Sadly, it stopped publication in 1996, but tried again as the *Ragged Edge* in January 1997. A Web site was launched at the same time, but it has had no new content since 2006. The print version of *Ragged Edge* ended in 2004. They simply ran out of money. The Advocado Press (advocadopress.

org) still sells a few books written by Johnson and others. If you want the flavor of the *Rag* go there and buy the book the *Ragged Edge*. If you want the text version of every *Rag* during its 1980 to 1996 run, that's there too. One thing is certain: Its defiant voice has been sorely missed.

> *Christ, Hoop, we could have used The Rag's voice in the most recent "better-off-dead" story. Ten pushes forward, a hundred steps back. Do tell.*

To begin with, this story is heartbreaking. I read the initial story on CNN.

Setting the stage is the first paragraph of CNN's story:

> It's a grim topic: What would you want if you were on life support after a life-altering accident? Would you want to live in a wheelchair, or would you want to die?

CNN went on to report that a young man fell out of a tree while deer hunting and broke his neck, quite severely in three places. This happened on a Saturday. The very next day he was brought out of a drug-induced coma and gave his consent to be removed from life support. Five hours later he died. The man was newly married and a father-to-be. He chose death.

Now, I don't have a problem with his right to choose, but I do think it was made far too soon. He was popped out of a coma and imme-diately gave his consent to be unplugged. Forget that he had to have been in shock and disoriented so soon after being injured, and that spinal cord injuries are unpredictable. Usually doctors wait for spinal-cord swelling to go down and prognoses can and do change daily and weekly. I certainly don't know the medical details, but it appears the man's main issue was the wheelchair. His wife was quoted as saying, "The last thing he wanted was to be in a wheelchair."

Ok, I get that. I felt exactly the same way as detailed in previous chapters, and so did a gentleman we will meet in the next chapter named Ed Roberts. The problem is: For many of us that fate-worse-than-death conviction was untrue. Putting all that aside, though, my main objection was the news coverage. As with the graveyard statue concept of better-off-dead, most Facebook people and those commenting on the CNN story agreed with the injured man's choice. It was completely rational to them, even brave, that death was the best choice. Others went so far as to judge and offer asinine opinions about the rest of us with disabilities like these few lines of puke:

Happy Mouths who insist you still have a life after your accident. The patients don't become "accepted of their situations" after ten years. They simply become resigned to the inevitable.

I cannot sit back and have this shit be seen as a legitimate broad-stroke truism because *it's a lie*! And worse, it marginalizes ALL people who use wheelchairs. These stupid, ignorant opinions vomit out onto the printed page like toxic waste.

The good news is that these assholes are saying what they really think. That candor surfaces when a controversial event like this hits the news, and/or when we with disabilities challenge such toxic attitudes.

The whole thing is an affront to my life and the lives of thousands and thousands of other people with disabilities. No way was I going to sit back and get pushed around by CNN and the McNasties weighing in on the story. Here is a Facebook thread with the names removed that illustrates how Spokes originally reacted to the story, and then how some replied:

Spokes This story sucks for people with disabilities. It feeds the stereotype that ALL of us in chairs would be better off dead. I don't know this man's circumstance just 1-2 days after his accident, but that sounds a bit soon to throw in the towel. And when the first paragraph of a CNN article asks, "Would you want to live in a wheelchair, or would you want to die?" That's a hard slap in my face and an insult to all the wonderful, happy people I know who use wheelchairs.

K: Shame on you for judging him. It was HIS choice. I'm sure YOU and your opinions were the last thing on his mind.

Spokes: Shaming itself is judging, K.

The shame belongs to those sensationalizing a story that stereotypes those of us who live happy lives with our disabilities. I in no way judge his choice, but I do judge these stories that judge our choice to live good, happy lives with disabilities, and only serve to reinforce the stereotypes that probably influenced this young man's decision. I too thought I'd be better off dead. It took time for me to realize that wasn't true - and for a vast majority. Time he will never have. The entire story saddens me. May he have peace.

F: This has nothing to do with you and your choice!!!

H: Being disabled and living with a breathing tube are two very different things. My uncle was paralyzed in a car accident at a young age and lived a fulfilling life. Living with a breathing tube who knows but he wouldn't have had lived as long or went to college, learn to drive and live on his own.

M: the guy has a choice, and he made it..not sure it has anything at all to do with anybody other then himself.

J: Instead of making this story about you maybe you should have read the entire article and understand what he was going to have to deal with. He chose to pull the plug because he was paralyzed and he would have had to have a breathing machine with him at all times. crushed 3 vertebrae. There was no fixing it. I hate it when people trying to make someone else's story about them and their sob story. boo hoo. It's not about you.

J: The entire article is a complete joke. His family making him understand that he will never hold his baby is a joke. Looks like they wanted him to die than rather him be a burden on them shame on them, and this stupid article.

Spokes When the first paragraph of a national article asks, "Would you want to live in a wheelchair, or would you want to die?" - it becomes about everyone who uses a wheelchair. For those of you who can't see that, no amount of explanation will ever get through.

Again, these are the proverbial tips of icebergs. The bergs themselves are huge. But Spokes got 64 "Likes" of people agreeing with what he was saying. Those pale in comparison to those who agreed that death is the way. But those 64 "Likes" give me hope, and keep me writing about my life with a disability.

My sympathy to this young man's family, and may he rest in peace.

So, that's that, Spokes. These are the times when we most miss the *Disability Rag.*

It really is, Hooper. These reactions remind me of this Sufi Tale:

> A man whom everyone had believed had died was placed in a coffin to be buried. But he was not dead and regained consciousness, lifting the coffin lid and crying for help. But the mourners replied that he could not be alive.
>
> "It's impossible," they said, "because the experts have declared him dead."
>
> The man protested: "I am alive!"
>
> A judge who was among the mourners said, "You have heard what the dead man has said. You mourners tell me what is true."
>
> "He's dead," said the mourners.
>
> "Bury him," said the experts.
>
> And thus the man was buried.

Spokes, funny, because that Sufi tale reminds me of the Monty Python musical *Spamalot* that Bunny and I saw on Broadway. Set during the great plague, the character Lance sees a thought-to-be-dead man, and tries to put him on the death wagon, and it leads into the song, "He Is Not Dead Yet." I guess I think of that here because, as the saying goes, if I don't laugh I'll cry. Here is the opening of that scene:

ROBIN (spoken):
Bring out your dead! Bring out your dead!

LANCE (spoken):
Here's one.

DAD (spoken):
I'm not dead!

ROBIN (spoken):
Here, he says he's not dead!

LANCE (spoken):
Yes he is.

DAD (spoken):
I feel happy. I feel happy.
(sung)
I am not dead yet
I can dance and I can sing
I am not dead yet
I can do the Highland Fling

I am not dead yet
No need to go to bed
No need to call the doctor
Cause I'm not yet dead.

No, Spokes, we are not dead yet.

Tell me again about Ed Roberts, Hooper. I won't say a word.

Ok, Spokes, but you know you can't keep your big mouth shut.

CHAPTER 10

INDEPENDENT LIVING

I f someone says independent living, I immediately say Ed Roberts. I spoke with Ed in the late '80s after the Hooper family moved to Sarasota, Florida. A dedicated group of people wanted to start an Independent Living Center in Sarasota. Roberts is the father of the independent living movement, so who better to talk to, I thought?

I first learned about Ed, like we did so many other disability activists, in the *Disability Rag*. For those who don't know anything about Ed Roberts, go to YouTube and find his *60 Minutes* interview with Harry Reasoner. It is a great eye-opener.

Roberts was one of the first to define independence outside physical parameters. He was about as physically disabled as one can get. Roberts contracted polio in 1953 at the age of 14 and was totally paralyzed feet to hands. He could move only two fingers and needed an iron lung to breathe. His doctor told his mother that both Roberts and she would be better off if Ed were dead. Sound familiar? And he was ready to die.

Years later Roberts said:

Well, I decided to die in the beginning. People told me basically that I would have no life. When you're in an iron lung and you're paralyzed from the neck down, in a hospital where their whole job is to save your life, you've got to be pretty creative to kill yourself.

Roberts decided to starve himself to death and came very close to succeeding. He was down to fifty pounds. My first wheelchair weighed more than fifty pounds. But something stirred him to live. He wasn't sure himself what, but something did, and every person with a severe disability—any disability—should be grateful that he did. His first dramatic choice was to *live* and he went on from there to help create the concept of independent living.

Roberts reasoned that independent living for a person with a disability is about controlling one's own life. You decide, he said. Now, that's not to say Roberts didn't believe in doing everything that you are physically capable of doing. He did. He himself learned to operate a power wheelchair, no small feat for his level of disability. But the more severe your disability, the more assistance you might need. Roberts needed personal care but it was he who directed that care. He was in charge, not the person actually providing the care. This was new. Also, Roberts demanded by his words and actions the same choices and control in his day-to-day life that his non-disabled peers had. He wanted to grow up with family, not in an institution. He wanted to go to the same schools, use the same buses, and work in the same jobs as everyone else. Sounds like a no-brainer now, but it wasn't back then. It was revolutionary. He also wanted a family of his own which as it turns out he had—a wife and a son.

Here's what Roberts himself said:

Independent Living is a psychological idea much more than a physical concept. I'm paralyzed from the neck down, but I am completely in control of my own life. I make decisions about what I want. And when you begin to believe that it is very empowering and powerful. And then it catches on with other people. They say, well, if he can do that, why can't I?

Ed Roberts died in 1995, but he left a legacy as both an activist and advocate for people with disabilities around the world. Here are just some of his accomplishments:

- Just like blacks who broke the color barrier at American universities in the 1960s led to nationwide integrated campuses, Robert's attendance at University of California Berkley was a first, and has paved the way for thousands, if not millions of others.
- In 1974, Congress passed the Education of the Handicapped Act guaranteeing an equal education for all children with disabilities. College campuses across the world are now implementing disability studies programs.
- The Persons with Disability Studies Program (PDSP) was the first program of its kind. Now almost every university and community college has a similar program, no longer restricted to students with physical disabilities.
- The Berkley Center for Independent Living was the first organization of its kind. There are now more than four hundred in the United States and many more across the world.
- Roberts became the first person with a disability of his significance to direct a state (California) Vocational Rehabilitation agency. Many more have followed in his wheelprints.
- The World Institute on Disability has grown from its beginnings of three founders (Roberts was one) in 1983 to an organization of dozens of employees known throughout the world for a multitude of activities.
- The MacArthur Fellowship has been awarded to other disability rights activists since Roberts received his in 1984.

Roberts' legacy may live on most fundamentally in the individuals he touched. At a memorial service held at World Institute on Disability shortly after Ed's death, a woman related the story of how her parents had moved to the United States from the Far East after she became disabled. She ended up in a hospital in the Bay Area wishing she were dead. When asked if she wanted anything she made a request to meet Ed. He visited. She related her story to him and he began to cry. When she saw his tears that he could not wipe from his face, she realized that she possessed physical capabilities that he did not. Yet he was a powerful, happy man in his huge, electronically-powered wheelchair, breathing with the aid of a respirator. She wondered why she was lying in a hospital bed. She got up. She has since become a well-known artist in the Bay Area.[10]

So many people with disabilities hear the negative messages—not the positive ones—either to their faces or in whispers and looks, those pitiful, sorrowful looks. And they give up. They become the very things they hear and learn, like a child who grows up being continually told he/she is worthless; deep down that child will probably feel worthless as adult.

This is not to say that life with a disability is a rosy, fairytale picture. People with disabilities *do* suffer and far too many want to die. Like aging, this disability shit isn't for sissies; it's tough both physically and emotionally. But much of that is learned from the outside in. Many live the stereotype instead of living their own lives. Roberts' life is a testament to the choice of living, and he became a "powerful, happy man." There are thousands of positive stories out there, but we don't hear them very often. Here are links to just three, or simply Google Dr. Ted Rummel, Tim Harris, and Stella Young TED:

http://www.dailymail.co.uk/news/article-2513994/Paralyzed-doctor-performs-surgery-thanks-stand-wheelchair.html#ixzz2maOL1ybG

---

10 http://www.independentliving.org/docs3/brown00a.html

http://www.amazingoasis.org/2013/12/restaurant-owner-with-down-syndrome.html

http://www.ted.com/talks/stella_young_i_m_not_your_inspiration_thank_you_very_much

Roberts was a key player in getting governmental funding and identifying what needed to comprise the core of Centers for Independent Living. Keeping the centers consumer-controlled was key to Roberts because it defined his basic premise: You are in charge.

Here's what defines federally funded Centers for Independent Living (CILs). It was set up to protect the integrity of Independent Living:

Definition of a Center for Independent Living from Section 702 of the Rehabilitation Act of 1973, as amended:

CENTER FOR INDEPENDENT LIVING- The term "center for independent living" means a consumer-controlled, community-based, cross-disability, nonresidential private nonprofit agency that is designed and operated within a local community by individuals with disabilities and provides an array of independent living services.

A Center for Independent Living:

51% of staff are persons with disabilities; 51% of Board of Directors are persons with disabilities; and provides four core services:

1. Information & referral
2. Independent living skills training

3. Individual and systems advocacy
4. Peer counseling[11]

So, what do you think of all that, Spokes? You still awake?

Of course, I'm awake. I love Ed Roberts! Hey, remember 87? That's the year we moved to Sarasota. Christ, that's 28 years ago. Ah, sun, fun. Retirement. Easy time.

Not exactly, Spokes.

No, not even close, Hoop. Sarasota is beautiful, but the access then was ugly. There was hardly a curb-cut in the entire downtown. You'd have thought with all the old bastards here the place would have been a little bit more wheelchair friendly.

Not so much, Spokes. By the way, we're now old bastards.

You are! Anyway, we started walking the wheelchair walk, Hoop. That's about the time we met Bill Knight. Wild Bill we called him.

Bill Knight is also a quad with the same disability rights philosophy as me, plus he had an incredible knack for advocating for causes like access. We teamed up and started a group called CURB (Citizens United to Remove Barriers) to bring attention to inaccessibility in Sarasota. It led to my first on-the-street protest.

We had tried to go through channels at city hall, but they fed us—and anyone else who tried to get wheelchair access—lip service. Bill was a master at getting to the right person and cutting through the bullshit. Not all the bureaucrats and politicians were unsympathetic to

---

11 http://www.ilru.org/html/publications/directory/index.html

our cause, and Knight somehow found those people and pleaded our case. He did it over and over again.

Our first effort was curb-cuts. We had some ears at city hall but not enough. We were getting a curb-cut here and a curb-cut there, but it was snail-slow. It would have taken thirty years at that rate! So, we decided to stage a protest down near the Social Security building. The cool part was that the city was actually putting in a curb-cut right there at Ringling and Orange, and we were invited to celebrate its completion. We used the event to protest and tell everyone who would listen that the whole town needed curb-cuts. The newspapers and TV picked up on it.

Gotta love sneaky, Fast Eddie. But we know the bureaucratic reply and refrain to that, don't we? "No Money! No Money in the budget."

That's right, money, money, money. With woe-is-them, forlorn looks on their faces, we would hear, where oh where were they ever going to get the money for these poor handicapped folks? Wheelchair users can't even get onto the city sidewalks and they were casting themselves as the ones who were in a bind.

It was BS, of course. They could find money for other worthwhile things like abstract art. Now, I love all kinds of art in our cities, towns, and parks. But a really big key for me loving public art is being able to get close enough to actually have a look. So, they could find money for that and many other things, but money for basic freedom and access for its disabled citizens was always hard to come by. It played like a shitty jingle I couldn't get out of my head: We don't have money in the budget for that. Our hands are tied.

Well, turns out they did have a funding source, one they never considered. And Knight found it. As I said, Knight had a knack. He discovered that the handicapped parking fine money was being used at the discretion of the city and county. In other words, you gimps get zip-a-dee-doo-dah. We thought, what better use for that money than funding curb cuts? Even the naysayers were silenced by that logic and as a result the entire downtown area was systematically made accessible.

Hey, Hooper, tell us about your favorite conservative blowhard and his take on curb cuts.

Ah, yes, R. Emmett Tyrrell, founder of the conservative *American Spectator* magazine and author of this compassionate bit of nasty where he castigates those he calls "career do-gooders" who "suddenly plowed up our sidewalks, leaving mischievous channels through which a solitary wheelchair might pass" while "in the meantime thousands of us stumble into the infernal depressions."

What a sweetheart this dude is, Hooper.

Tyrrell was my first exposure to far-right political thinking and how it affected the disability community. These guys were against anything that might actually help folks in need, and historically that includes so many other social programs people of this ilk opposed—like National Parks, Woman's suffrage, minimum wage, Social Security, Medicare and Medicaid, Civil Rights, Food Stamps, the EPA, Obamacare, etc. The list is almost as big as their smirks.

But I do love the honesty of Tyrrell. Like the Facebook folks in Chapter Nine, we know where he stands. He's a viper. He was not only against making sidewalks accessible; he didn't want to be reminded of our "infernal depressions"—as if he knew anything about us. I could never get my head around the ethics and maliciousness of a man who would deny another access to a sidewalk. And I always wonder how these folks sleep at night, and then bang, it comes to me: Assholes never have their days ruined; they ruin other people's days unless it somehow costs them money, like a handicapped parking fine, for example. Then the anger, ranting, and whining begin in earnest.

So, Sarasota and thousands of towns and cities across the US cut the curbs and made sidewalks wheelchair accessible. And guess what? Those towns and cities are thrilled. The sidewalks now have wheelchairs rolling on them, bringing money into local businesses. Those businesses in turn made their establishments accessible. Plus, those vilified curb-cuts provide communities major bonuses: giving easier access to emergency service, delivery people, strollers, shopping carts, blind people, those with joint problems, canes, and you name it. Like automatic doors, these so-called "mischievous channels" actually made everything better. Accessibility started to become the norm.

Turns out that the mean-spirited, flippant Tyrrell was wrong, but he happily poisoned the minds of his readers and perpetuated the stereotype. Even though it wasn't true, people believed and agreed with him. Still do.

Hoop, I have no doubt Tyrrell and the Nasty McNastingtons like him sleep like babies. What bugs me is those grins, those self-righteous grins. When the Far Right is happy like they are now after the 2014 elections, those grins are bigger than ever and are a smirky omen of funding cuts to those who need governmental help.

They all do seem to be excellent smirkers, Spokes.

Knight and I next turned our attention to Ed Smith Stadium, then the spring training facility for the Chicago White Sox. The City of Sarasota was building it and Knight found out that the wheelchair accessibility was inadequate. At the eleventh hour, we were able to work with the city to make changes that made both the restrooms and the stadium-seating more wheelchair accessible. Instead of the assigned birds-of-a-feather seating in one arbitrary area, we were able to have seating choices for wheelchair-users on the first and third base sides, behind the plate, and even some outfield seating. Nothing like a beer and a dog on a sunny Sarasota Saturday, watching a game from the seat of your wheelchair and singing "Take Me Out To The Ballgame."

We were on a roll (cliché and pun intended) so Knight and I started looking at Sarasota Country buses and bus stops. We were far from pioneers in this arena. There was and is an organization called ADAPT[12] that paved the way for mandatory accessible buses in the US. ADAPT is still active, fighting now to keep people with disabilities out of nursing homes. For over 30 years, they have been strong, take-it-to-the-streets activists and advocates (adapt.com). If you want tough, call ADAPT.

When Knight found out that the county was getting ready to replace some buses, we wrote a letter to the county commissioners basically saying that installing lifts on the new buses was not only the right thing to do, but also that as soon as the American with Disabilities Act (ADA)[13] is passed, accessible buses will be mandated. To our delight, the county agreed and purchased the new buses with lifts in 1989, a full year or more before the ADA was passed. It's worth pointing out that the far right politicians of that time (who in 2015 would be considered moderate) were against the ADA, saying it would open the floodgates to lawsuits. Also, that it would cost too much. Those forecasted lawsuits never flooded anything, of course, but the ADA—signed by moderate Republican George H W Bush—literally opened the doors to mainstream American life to many. Yes, that freedom did cost taxpayers and companies money. Freedom isn't cheap, though, is it? Many beneficiaries of the ADA were/are disabled veterans who

---

12 Originally ADAPT was American Disabled for Accessible Public Transportation and later American Disabled for Attendant Programs Today

13 http://www.accessiblesociety.org/topics/ada/

risk their lives and limbs so that the Mr. Tyrrell's of the world could have the freedom to spit out their bile. I couldn't find anywhere that Tyrrell himself had ever served in the military. I'm sure he didn't want to march into any of those freedom-giving "infernal depressions" he hissed at. He *is* getting older, however, and odds are getting better and better that he will join the ranks of those depressed handicapped folks he railed against.

Knight and I figured that the buses were going to be accessible, but how about the bus stops? Just a cursory look at a few stops clearly showed that they were woefully inaccessible and that all stops needed to be looked at. The county didn't want to inspect anything because they knew full well the stops would not pass, so Bill and I got into my car with the bus schedule of routes and went all through Sarasota County. We spent a week going from stop-to-stop making note of each stop's state of accessibility.

It wasn't pretty. Most bus stops were totally inaccessible, begging the question, "What good is an accessible bus if someone who uses a wheelchair can't get to it?" We had accessible buses that no one could access. Ridership would be down and the naysayers would say, "See, told you so. The handicapped don't want public transportation. They never use it." But these "If it helps people, I'm against it" McNasties of the world said the same thing about so-called "handicapped parking." These days I can scarcely find accessible parking. That's partly because every Tom, Dick, and Mary with a stubbed toe to a bum knee seems to have an accessible parking placard. Some need it. Others don't. (More on this aggravating problem in Chapter Thirteen).

To mitigate the "they never use it" argument, we wrote up a huge report identifying the bus stops, what the problems were, and rec- ommendations on how to fix each. Some just needed to be moved; they were adjacent to roadside ditches, for example. We compiled the report and brought it down to the county. As far as we know, not much was ever done with our report. Some stops were fixed, most were not. Knight told me months later that he saw the report collecting dust on the floor in a corner when he was visiting the County Manager.

To this day, there is an occasional news story about inaccessible bus stops in Sarasota County. The County quickly points out that a good number of bus stops are rural-like. It's not like a big city because a lot of our roads are without sidewalks. That's no excuse, though, for not doing all they can to make stops more accessible, and, then, most importantly, to actually inform people that they are accessible. Because without accessible bus stops disability ridership will always be low, and with that low ridership the Tyrrells of our world will be there to say over and over that the lifts on the buses cost too much and are unnecessary because no one uses them. We must be always watchful of those who want to take away our right to be in mainstream society.

Next up was the Van Wezel Performing Arts Hall built in 1968 and 1969 when wheelchair accessibility was not even a twinkle of consideration in the eye of architectural design. William Wesley Peters of Taliesin Associated Architects of the Frank Lloyd Wright Foundation conceived Van Wezel's seashell design. This design actually came from two seashells from the Sea of Japan, which are permanently displayed in the Hall. But its unique lavender and purple color scheme was selected by Wright's widow, Olgivanna Lloyd Wright, and has helped to make the building a Sarasota landmark.

Now, the stadium seating design in Van Wezel was great for able-bodied audiences, but not for people with disabilities. By 1990, Knight had become chairman of the City of Sarasota's Handicapped Advisory Board. I, too, was a member. Because the hall was literally poured in concrete and the restrooms were designed 100% inaccessible, to retrofit and make Van Wezel accessible was extraordinarily difficult. But through the efforts of the city and the advisory board lead by Knight, Van Wezel made the changes and has made many improvements since. I've been there quite a few times over the years, and although there are not a lot of seating-area options, I've always had a good experience there access-wise. When I go inside, I always think about Bill Knight and all the tireless work he did for people with disabilities in Sarasota.

It was time for a bigger step. Mike Garr, a rehab professional, came to me and asked if I would chair an effort to start a center for independent living. We had just started a wheelchair rugby team (see Chapter Eleven) in Sarasota and that was challenging, but it was time for me to start rolling the roll so-to-speak, and I agreed to chair the group that started the center. Turns out, this group was the best. These were super-hardworking, dedicated people—conscientious professionals and consumers who saw a huge need for a Center for Independent Living (CIL) in Sarasota. Some of us wanted a consumer database for personal caregivers—a safe, trustworthy source for people with disabilities to choose from, like the Berkley California CIL[14] program that is still operational in 2015. Others wanted a place for people after rehab to learn basic skills to live in the world: cooking, cleaning, banking, and other activities of daily living (ADLs). We all wanted a solid information and referral resource. Foremost, though, we all wanted a place that would advocate for people with disabilities, a place that would stand with them and behind them to ensure their full inclusion in our community.

So, I called Ed Roberts. I had an amazing conversation with him about Independent Living and its great potential. I asked for any advice in our efforts to start one. He said be prepared to work hard, but most of all "watch out for the bureaucrats." How prophetic that turned out to be.

The center was something that fit our goals perfectly. Our board included some of the hardest working people I'd ever been around

---

14 http://www.cilberkeley.org/personal-attendant-referrals/

in my life. They cared deeply and worked their asses off to build a foundation: We scrounged up seed money, got a local accountant to volunteer his time to apply for non-profit status, and wrote the bylaws. After tons of hard work, the Suncoast Center for Independent Living (SCIL) was incorporated in 1990 and then funded by the federal and state government as a CIL in 1991.

Our first director was a quad by the name of—surprise!—Bill Knight. That choice seemed so appropriate. Our board was made up of a cross-section of able-bodied and disabled people who had independence and advocacy at their core: Don, Laura, Gerry, Dennis, Barbara, Mike, and me as chairman/president. Mike left the board shortly after recruiting me due to work commitments. They were all fantastic.

One of the first things that Knight started was the ramp-building program. Many residents of Sarasota and Manatee counties had no independent access to where they lived. SCIL created a need-based program so people could get a ramp they otherwise couldn't afford to give them access in and out of their own homes. SCIL partnered with Home Depot and volunteer groups in Sarasota and Manatee Counties to fund and build the ramps.

Knight, the best advocate for disability issues around, was off to a great start. The ramp program was wildly successful, and SCIL started a loaner closet and then an equipment repair shop. These coupled with peer support and classes starting for activities for daily living completed and exceeded the four core services required for CIL funding. All was well. After four years as chairman/president, I left the center's board to what I thought was a healthy future for SCIL.

Sometime during the following ten years the center got sick: the able-bodied bureaucratic flu. It lost its way. It probably started when Bill Knight left in the mid-nineties. The consummate advocate was gone, and an able-bodied person replaced Knight. The center system-atically became more and more about money and less and less about the Ed Roberts' philosophy of independent living. The ebb contin-ued until at some point, money ruled. Slowly, it became fashionable to recruit movers and shakers (mostly able-bodied folks) who had no knowledge of Ed Roberts or his passion and dream. By 2003, not one board member, not one staff member even knew who Ed Roberts was!

How did money affect SCIL and many, many other CILs across the country? It effectively pulled the teeth of advocacy. Where Bill Knight would insist, confront, prod, cajole, and even embarrass powers-that-be to do the right thing—the post-Knight SCIL would *always* remain silent if they thought there was *any* chance that it might rub anyone the wrong way: city, county, state, feds, or private entity. SCIL wasn't alone in that approach. The need for money became competitive even among sister CILs because centers around Florida were after the same block of gov-ernment bucks. The dilemma for them was: lose your funding, lose your job, lose your center. That paranoia, that dependence on government funding, was a hole that got deeper and deeper. Ironically, the centers for independent living themselves became dependent and servants to money and corporate lobbying. The powerful nursing home lobby, for example, has no interest in people with disabilities living independently. Those lobbyists work behind the scenes with politicians to find ways to pull or reduce the funding on CILs advocating for better treatment inside assisted living facilities. And there are many people with disabilities that DO NOT need to live in a nursing home. So the last thing nursing home lobbyists want is for CILs to actively advocate and facilitate removing people from institutional living. That's the dream CILs were supposed to be advocating and fighting for, and that's the dream the nursing home lobby was/is trying to squash.

When CILs don't actively advocate for people with disabilities, they lose far more than money. What non-advocacy CILs lose is credibility and respect from the many good people in government they sought to appease. And, they lose the trust of the people with disabilities they are supposed to be serving. Worse and ultimately, though, they sell out a philosophy they either don't understand or don't think is worth fighting for. A book could be written on the money issue alone.

It's important to say that there are still many centers in the US that carry the Ed Roberts' philosophy in their hearts and advocate the way he would have. Roberts would be most proud of each of them. Berkeley (cilberkeley.org) immediately comes to mind, but find what works for you. You'll know quite soon after contacting them where the center's priorities lie. When in doubt, ask ADAPT. They will know. They have a photo of Ed Roberts prominently displayed on their web page. Every CIL in the world should also have a photo of Roberts as reminder of what this independent living movement is all about.

In late 2003, Dawkins, who has supplemented and refreshed many of my memories on this debacle, contacted me about returning to the SCIL board. I screwed up and said yes.

Hey, Hoop, I'm back. Did I miss anything?

I was talking about returning to the SCIL board.

Oh, boy, you sure got that stuck in your ass.

Sure did. Me and lots of others.

I remember my very first meeting. The board was in the final stages of approving a construction plan for a SCIL building. I asked, why would you want to spend your time and resources building a building? Keep renting, I suggested. They all looked at me like I shot their dog. Not one person at that table thought the new building was a bad idea.

I thought it was a terrible idea. CILs don't own and build buildings; they build independence. I wondered: How the hell do you pay for it? How will the core services suffer? They said they had a fund (that sounded shady, but we were assured it was legit) and that services would not be affected. How, I thought? The motion passed and so, too, did the slow spiral down the tubes.

Originally they told Dawkins that the building would have a community center, even a gym. As Dawkins now says, "They played me." Trouble is, none of those good intentions made it into the final building plans. I hated the whole thing. And everyone on the board knew it. I probably should have resigned on the spot, but I made a commitment. Moreover, the center was built on the backs of good people who sacrificed hundreds and hundreds of hours of their time to make something special happen. I owed it to them, so I worked in good faith to make it all work, even on that stupid damned building.

This first order of business in my mind was to get the people who worked at SCIL familiar with Ed Roberts. Without him, they would all be working elsewhere or perhaps not at all. So, using photos of SCIL clients and the Roberts' *60 Minute* interview with Harry Reasoner, I put together a video (about 14 minutes long) so we could show people what CILs stood for and where they came from. First, the staff needed to see it, and then we could use it for potential clients, family, building donors, board members, and potential board members. To my mind it was required viewing. The staff watched the video first, and afterward I gave them a brief overview of Ed Roberts, *the father of independent living*. They seemed impressed although none knew of Ed Roberts.

I was excited and energized, until the director of the center came up to me and said, "That was pretty good, Ed—a little long, though. Who was Roberts again?" I'm rarely speechless, but this floored me. The Ed Roberts interview took up 80% of the run time and was worth every frame to understand the core philosophy of the CIL movement. Our own director was clueless even after looking at the face and hearing the voice of the man who started it all. To me, it was like an American not knowing George Washington. (And like the bus stop report, the video that I spent many hours putting together would sit and collect dust). I knew right then that I either needed to walk away from SCIL, or try to change everything and get back the CIL we founded, the Ed Roberts model.

Dawkins and I chose change. What we didn't know was that the director and key board members were planning changes of their own. For example, we were reworking the SCIL brochure, updating it. At a board meeting, a motion was made that we remove Advocacy from the brochure. Dawkins and I about flipped over backwards in our wheelchairs. At first we tried to reason with these folks saying that the very heart and soul of independent living is advocacy—without it, it's another social service agency. Sadly and incredibly, that did not resonate with them. Money did. So we also argued that if we eliminate one of the core services—advocacy!—we would not be eligible for government funding. *That* hit home. The motion was withdrawn, but not their intent to abandon even the pretense of advocacy. They were against advocacy; and *never* really practiced it. Tensions grew.

Little did we know that around that same time an effort was started by some Washington D.C. governmental employees with disabilities to actually remove advocacy as one of the requirements for core CIL services. Dawkins and I later called them Uncle Tims. These were George W. Bush appointees whose goal was to dismantle the CIL paradigm championed by Ed Roberts. It was all in serious danger. The no-funding message to CILs was clear and simple: You rock the boat; we'll sink your boat.

This ignited the passions of real CIL folks across the county who knew precisely who Ed Roberts was. Led by the National Council on

Independent Living (NCIL), they shut the misguided effort down. But even after a big win, the defenders of the Ed Roberts' brand of independent living must be ever vigilant because lobbying and money-driven ideology never take a day off. And it's why people with disabilities must vote locally and nationally. If the wrong people get into power, which they just now have in the 2014 elections, our independence can be taken with a pen stroke. We not might be able to walk, see, hear, or speak, but we are all able to vote.

Please Vote!

On the local front, there was some good news: SCIL's director was retiring. Dawkins and I immediately got on the search committee to find a replacement. It was a three-person committee because most board members didn't want to do detail work, and after going through tons of resumes and doing interviews we found our guy. Well, Dawk and I found our guy. The other committee member didn't like the candidate, but could never articulate why. "Just a gut feeling," we were told. But it was 2 to 1.

The man we hired was able-bodied but had a strong, successful record as an activist-driven director of a CIL. His philosophy was grounded in the Ed Roberts' model of independent living. He actually knew who Ed Roberts was and what he stood for. Dawk and I were elated!

However, that third committee member wasn't happy at all. Any boat-rocking advocacy that might hinder getting donations and governmental building-code support for the building he championed was unacceptable. He was the most influential board member and he wanted to keep the status quo with someone from the inside running the center. This resentment immediately permeated the staff and most of the board. Our new director didn't feel welcome; he felt the resentment. How could he not?

But the new director didn't help himself by openly stating his political and personal beliefs. He was against the war in Iraq before most Americans were, and was a pacifist who spoke openly about it, which further alienated him from SCIL staffers and board members. He later told Dawkins and me that he thought being against war was a good thing that his new co-workers would understand and respect. Wrong! Also, at that same time Dawkins and I were being labeled as rebels and crazies for standing up for advocacy and independent living and for hiring a director who stood for the same. The irony of that makes me want to laugh and scream at the same time.

Now, if you are in a workplace where everyone is focused on finding mistakes in your work, mistakes will be found—fabricated and/or exaggerated. And under this pressure you cannot operate openly and freely. This was the trap our new director found himself trying to avoid, and sure enough he misstepped. Our director used a SCIL van to help a friend move some personal stuff, and all hell broke loose. The dogs could smell blood. (But there was a far bigger stink in the back corners of SCIL that wouldn't be uncovered for another year or so.)

Misappropriation of property was the topic of our special meeting, all contrived and set up in advance by influential board members, mostly able-bodied. I found out first hand that day the definition of a Kangaroo Court. A good man was sent packing—not immediately but the die was cast. Soon after, at 50-years-old, his name besmirched and his career destroyed, he was forced out. Dawkins and I argued that the use of a van without consent was an oversight but not grounds for dismissal and placing a permanent black mark on a man's record. We also said to the blank faces and glazed-over eyes that these types of usages go on all the time. It's called a helping-hand using the company truck. No arguing would have convinced these folks, though; they decided on dismissal long before they entered the room. Initially the director denied the usage, fearing it would be used against him. And, of course, it was. Dawkins and I to this day look back at this as the saddest, most frustrating and shameful experience of our lives with a disability. (I saw our ousted director about seven years after this travesty. He had not regained his previous employment stature and still hadn't found a fulltime job.)

It was time to fight, to really fight for what we had started 15 years earlier. Political fighting is exhausting, especially if you are otherwise employed or busy. Board elections were coming up and I decided to run for president again. Behind the scenes things were getting ugly. In person, we smiled at one another. Our side's nastiness was centered on SCIL drifting away from base CIL philosophy. We wanted to clean house. We said that the center had lost itself in money and that too much time was being spent on the SCIL building. It was time to reclaim the roots of advocacy. It was a clear threat to everything the opposition stood for, so the other camp went down and dirty personal. They called Dawkins and me names. I was reckless, a dictator, they said. Dawk was my attack dog. SCIL would lose everything, they said.

The election was a couple of months away and the votes were a solid 5 to 5 with one undecided. That undecided person was a person with a disability so we thought he was a shoe in for our side. Dawkins and I spoke to him on the phone a lot about CILs and what they were all about, and Dawk gave him rides to meetings and appointments. The other guys bought him breakfast and lunch once or twice a week, and filled his head with doom and gloom about how we would destroy the center and its new building. Evidently the way to a man's vote is through fear and through his stomach. We lost 6–5. I resigned from the board November 3, 2005—Dawk shortly thereafter. Dawkins and I had no contact with the center after resigning. We failed, and we both felt that loss deeply.

A little over a year later, a longtime SCIL employee was arrested for embezzlement of $85,000. Turns out that that employee was also the primary insider working to dump the director that Dawkins and I brought in because, guess what, he was asking to see the books. We think the idea to embezzle SCIL money probably came from the way monies were diverted into the building fund. It was easy because no one questioned the bookkeeping. There had to have been red flags, but except for the ousted director, no one asked. Turns out the then president and the old director were clueless of a crime going on right before their eyes, not guilty of anything except the incompetence of tunnel vision. Board members scattered like blown leaves after that arrest.

When money is the only foundation on what you build, it will likely build the conditions for corruption and collapse. I don't think these were devious people (except the embezzler). Their intentions were good, but they were not doing the real work of independent living; they merely went through the motions. The actual service providers inside SCIL cared deeply and did their work diligently with the other core services. But the board and managing staff lost its way in a search for money and the misguided need for some trophy building, instead of operating a fulltime work hub for independence and advocacy for people with disabilities.

What of that grand building? Well, the building fund money ($50,000 or so) was used to get it started in 2004 and it was finished in 2005. The plan was to get a mortgage and to fundraise. They got the mortgage but not much else. SCIL was only big enough to occupy half the space, so the other half would be rented to help cover the mortgage payment. 2007 rolled around, the embezzlement hit, then the economic collapse of 2008, and all that remained was a white elephant sitting on 2989 Fruitville Road. Recently, the building was sold as a short-sale after a foreclosure judgment against SCIL. Initially, much was made over the stolen money and the total loss of services for people who needed day-to-day help or ramps or information, but that was quickly swept under the carpet to avoid embarrassment, I guess. For me, I think of all the services lost because of that building—the diverted building fund money. The embezzled $85,000! I think of that director who lost his job and reputation. I think of the utter time-wasting, service-sucking preoccupation with that freaking building. I think of those founders and of Mike Garr who died in 2002. I think of how it all went to shit, and it makes me sick to my stomach.

SCIL itself survived somehow, and now successfully operates from a rented office in Sarasota. If you go to SCIL's Facebook page or its web site there will be no mention of me as its founding chairman and first president, or of Dawkins, or of all those other founders, with exception of Mike Garr who facilitated the seed idea. They probably don't even know who I am, and that's fine as long as they know who Ed Roberts is and what he stood for. I hope they do because it's not really a CIL without that.

"Watch out," Roberts said all those years earlier. Can't say I wasn't warned.

A very sad end to this chapter: I found out a week before the final draft of *Don't Push Me* that Bill Knight passed away in early 2014. I had been trying unsuccessfully for months to contact him after his Facebook page suddenly vanished. There are tons of Bill Knights out there, so I almost gave up. I finally found him by Googling "William Knight Centers for Independent Living" and his obituary popped up and smacked me in the face. After the shock, it felt "right" that I discovered Bill's passing by searching "independent living." He was a fierce advocate of independence—who walked the wheelchair walk—for people with disabilities. Rest in peace, my friend.

CHAPTER 11

MURDERBALL

The practice of sport is a human right. Every individual must have the possibility of practicing sport, without discrimination of any kind and in the Olympic spirit, which requires mutual understanding with a spirit of friendship, solidarity and fair play.

– Olympic Charter

Nick
by Don Dawkins

Don Dawkins is a longtime friend and independent living advocate and activist who worked most of his life as a Recreational Therapist. This is his story about Nick:

I met him one winter morning. He had been admitted to our Spinal Cord Injury (SCI) unit the night before. As a department head I read his history, reviewed his meds, and went down the hall to meet him. Like so many before him he was lying on his back in a halo head-and-neck brace in obvious pain. Ever meet someone you click with instantaneously? That's the way it was with Nick and I, right from the start.

He was 17—a surfer and soccer player from Venice, Florida. Grew up on the beach. His Father had committed suicide when Nick was 4. His Mother had trouble with booze and men. He had a very close-knit group of friends. They grew up together and raised each other, and they were fiercely protective of one another. It touched me as it reminded me of my boyhood buddies. He was an easy kid to like: Funny, quiet, good looking with a mischievous grin. All of us on the SCI team loved him from the get go. He was the patient you dream of: competitive, could take the pain, and loved to be pushed. In short he was a jock with a strong sense of self.

One of the first things you do in rehab is get them up on a tilt table to begin the process. With a cervical spinal cord injury the sympathetic nervous system is greatly affected and blood pressures will fluctuate when you begin to sit patients up. The tilt table stands them and begins this process. At first Nick could only tolerate about 40 degrees. Many times patients will pass out. It can be terrifying for some. We would get Nick up and see him fading. The protocol is to talk them through it, try to keep them conscious. He would stay on it for a few minutes and pass out. Karen, the PT, would pinch the hell out of his earlobe to use pain stimulation to bring him back. He would wake, look at us and say, "Dudes be cool with my ear," and we would all laugh, including him.

He was on the unit for five months. Reggae music would blare from his room. His friends hung out constantly. As a rehab team we loved it and so did the other SCI patients. Even though he was a fresh injury his leadership stood out even then. He had his moments of despair and depression, so he and I had many, many discussions about life and its harsh realities. He loved mocking me, calling me the "King of clichés." As a professional I had been trained to keep a distance, *do not* get close, but I broke that rule with Nick. I had this bond with him, and he with me. That had never happened to me before in my work world and never would again.

After a few months the halo came off and we began pushing him hard physically. He ate it up. Some days he would hardly be able to push his chair at the end of the day and every muscle he could feel would ache, but he never complained. In fact, when I would ask how he felt, he would grin and tell me to "bring it, dude." We had started a wheelchair sports program the Hospital sponsored. It was protocol to expose patients to adaptive recreation as both a way to increase physicality and regain their sense of self. It is an amazing thing to see young men and women regain confidence and self esteem after a catastrophic injury through some form of recreation. It was in the early spring when I scheduled Nick to attended and participate in a quad rugby practice at Arlington Recreation Center's gym.

If you grow up around sports and love playing sports, a cata-strophic spinal cord injury may rob you of your identity. It is as common as a cold in a physical rehabilitation setting. My SCI teammate Joey, an OT, and I loaded Nick up into the rehab hospital van for the ten-minute ride to the practice facility.

As I drove the van up Tuttle Road I looked in the mirror at Nick, and asked. "Whattaya say bud, excited about going to practice?"

"You want me to tell you the truth?" he said quietly.

"I always want you to tell me the truth," I replied.

"It's a bunch of cripples bouncing a ball," he said.

I was stunned. That was exactly what I had told my sister thirty-five years before when she mentioned wheelchair basketball to me. We finished the ride in silence.

If you think you have lost something and then regain it, it's a powerful and many times an overwhelming feeling. Going into that gym, hearing the sound and echoes of shouts and bouncing balls, even the smell is a surreal experience. I introduced Nick to everyone, got him in a rugby chair, and showed him how to strap himself up. He had already watched tapes with me about rugby so he understood the basic fundamentals. I never expected much from a new injury at their first practice and neither did the other older and experienced wheelchair athletes. Nick blew us all away. He took to that game like the proverbial duck to water. It was a two-hour practice. I didn't expect him to hang with us but he did. His competitive instincts awakened and he blew us away with his natural abilities. At the end he was exhausted but obviously excited and happy.

Everyone climbs back into their street chairs and we take Nick back out to the van. Put him on the lift and tie him down inside. I climb into the drivers seat and begin the ride back to the hospital.

As we are bumping along on Tuttle Road, I looked at him in the mirror and asked "How about it Nicky, is this sports?" To the day I die I will never forget the look on this tough kid's face, who was in the middle of a hell very few can ever understand. He looked back at me in the mirror and quietly said "yeah," and burst into tears. Not tears of shame or regret but tears of joy. He had realized, like thousands of others of us had, that you are not defined by ambulating. You are defined by what is in your heart.

Nick went on to play quad rugby on a national level and began to rebuild his life. He struggled like we all did in the beginning. I once went to his house at 2 a.m. and took a 357 magnum away from him and a bottle of Jack Daniels. He lost a girl he loved very much, but he didn't know quit. He became very close to his grandparents and was rebuilding his life.

He played for Sarasota for a couple of years and was recruited by a rugby program in Austin, Texas, and he moved there. They won a National Championship in 2004. We talked the night of that win and he was so happy, making plans to attend a Community College. A week later he was dead. He drowned in a swimming accident on a tubing trip celebrating the big win with his teammates.

I loved Nick and mourn him to this day—always will. He was a free spirit and a strong life force. Here's what consoles me. He regained his self-esteem and identity, his sense of self. That's the beauty of sport; that's the wonder of athletics.

God bless you little brother you are missed and we will meet again.
-end

Hundreds and hundreds of quads have had their lives changed because of quad rugby, originally Murderball. Nick turned his life completely around, and then he suddenly and tragically died, proving again how life can be so unrelentingly unfair. We all knew Nicky, played rugby with him, he became family, we laughed with him, we loved him. He's part of our team's fabric and quad rugby's story—a brother lost far too soon.

Murderball itself was made quasi-famous by the movie of the same name. I urge everyone to see this movie. Here's why from my 2005 review:

Murderball
Academy Award Nomination
Documentary
Directed by Henry Alex Rubin, Dana Adam Shapiro.
85 minutes, Rated R

Murderball is getting rave reviews from critics like Roger Ebert of the Chicago Sun-Times, who predicts an Oscar for it for best documentary. It already won both the Sundance Audience Choice Award and the Special Jury Award for editing.

But the critics got one thing wrong: *Murderball* doesn't dispel myths and stereotypes. It takes big fat bites out of those sugary sweet, pathetic images and stereotypes, chews 'em up and spits 'em out. It's not a magic pill that will make pity and stereotypes go away, but it is quite simply the best film ever made on disability.

It amazes me that these filmmakers were able to render such an honest portrayal of living life from the seat of a wheelchair. Somehow, either by the sheer exposure to the people or by some innate understanding, directors Henry Alex Rubin and Dana Adam Shapiro "got it," and this film is a joy to watch, especially the way we did, with family and about twelve other quads. Plus, we knew these guys in the film, played with and against them.

This movie is funny. It is sad. It is fiery, fast, frank, explosive, sexy, tender, loving, and the action is bone-jarring, just like quad rugby, aka Murderball.

The music is perfect. The editing superb.

What more could you ask for? How about an obsessive villain, Joe Soares (who was at our screening), and a scary-looking good guy, Mark Zupan, who looks like he just jumped out of the X-Games, tattoos and all? Soares left Team USA when he wasn't chosen to be on the 2000 Paralympic team; out of revenge he became the coach of Team Canada. This prompted some Team USA members to call Soares a traitor. Zupan said, "I wouldn't piss on him if he was on fire." Game on!

That's the underlying conflict that drives *Murderball* to its conclusion: USA vs. Canada, Soares vs. Zupan and every member of Team USA.

But there's a much higher message coming out of this movie, because the filmmakers focused on the people. Even Soares is softened in the end, thank God.

Zupan, Andy Cohen, and Scott Hogsett are in reality articulate, good-natured guys, quite different from their rugby personas. They have wry, sarcastic senses of humor, and they want gold, not hugs. They want women, not mommies. And they succeed. Women love quads, and we love women. Women see quads as safe and exciting because there's an instinctive curiosity women have about how "things work." If they get too curious, they find out exactly how things work. Anyway, those "rugby faces" on Zupan, Cohen, and Hogsett we see at tournaments don't seem to be who those guys are at all. So that insight is refreshing.

Then there's Bobby Lujano, who comes off just like, well, Bobby Lujano. His scenes are poignant, powerful, thought-provoking. When his father hugs him after the USA loses to Canada in Athens, the love leaps off of the screen and into your heart. If you're a softy like me, you will cry.

Murderball also follows a newly injured guy, Keith Cavill. His portrayal had me flashing back on my early days of re-hab. Watching his ride home from rehab, with his quad hand stuck out the window feeling the scary air of freedom, was emotional. We'd all had that same feeling: "Ok, I'm out, but now what? I'm screwed." It's painful to watch him go through what every new spinal cord injury goes through, but that's what shapes us. That's what makes us strong or that's what breaks us.

In a scene later in the film, Zupan visits the rehab center and puts Cavill into his rugby chair. Cavill lights up for the first time since his injury. He spins around and gets the feel. He wants to hit something. He feels free. He feels hope. All the while, a physical therapist is telling him to be careful; he's too fragile. (Quads in the movie theater watching this scene just laughed.) Zupan comes up to him; Cavill inches forward, then lightly bumps Zupan's everyday chair. You can tell he wants to give Zupan a good solid whack. A quad rugby player is born.

Finally, there is Chris Igoe, whom I met at the screening and liked instantly. Zupan and Igoe were best friends. After the drunken accident that broke Zupan's neck, Igoe blamed himself. The two became estranged, Igoe nearly suicidal with guilt. Igoe has finally forgiven himself, he told me. And Zupan feels that getting injured was the best thing that's happened to him (His reaction is not uncommon among quads who have survived and carved out a life for themselves.). Their reconciliation on-screen is quite moving.

Murderball is about winning and losing. It's about driven athletes. But it's mostly about survival and moving forward after one is injured. It's about people, people who succeed and people who fail. Sound familiar? It's about life.

In real life, it doesn't have to be quad rugby—you can find your passion and pursue your dreams with any sport or work or art. It's whatever motivates you. You can move past the devastation of being severely injured and live a happy, fulfilling life.

If you able-bodied folks want to get some inkling of what living with a disability is like, go see *Murderball*. You'll learn more in 85 minutes than you could in a lifetime of politically correct "education." This movie is that good.
-end

Well, Spokes, it lost the Oscar to *March of the Penguins.*

I know! Penguins, fucking penguins! Quads don't waddle and aren't as cute, I guess, but shit, Hooper, penguins? So what, they marched 75 miles to mate? Hell, I'd roll 150 miles for sex.

Calm down, Ableman. As I was saying…

Murderball itself was invented in Canada. A group of quadriplegic athletes were sick and tired of riding the bench and playing second fiddle in wheelchair basketball, which was dominated by paraplegics and amputees. So, using a volleyball, they started playing a little game of "kill the guy with the ball." It started as keep-away, and it slowly evolved into what those good hockey-loving Canadians called Murderball, or "kill the guy with the ball" with rules. The game is played on a basketball-sized court with goals on each end. Go to quadrugby.com for details.

Murderball first appeared outside of Canada in 1979, and by 1988 was being played in various cities in the US under its new corporate-friendly name Quad Rugby. The United States Quad Rugby Association (USQRA) was formed in 1988 to regulate play and the first National Tournament was played that same year. Internationally the sport is called Wheelchair Rugby because varying other disability types are eligible as long as they have dysfunction in all four limbs. But most old-school, spinal-cord-injured quads still prefer the sport be called quad rugby or Murderball. It honors the game's roots.

There are tons of rules now, but the basics are the same as the original Murderball:

- Each team has 4 players who play both offense and defense with bench subs available.
- Full wheelchair contact.
- 1 point awarded to a player who crosses the goal line with the ball.
- Dribble every ten seconds or it's a turnover.
- No personal contact such as slapping, punching, biting off ears, gouging out eyes, etc., or it's off to the penalty box (Canadians!).

The greatest aspect of Murderball is inclusion. You can be an athlete again, or perhaps for the first time. Quads were excluded from many sport's opportunities because of their physical limitations, and the farther up the cervical injury ladder you go, the more physically disabled you become. So a classification system was established and refined over the years to assign a point value according to one's function. The lowest value and function is .5, the highest 3.5. Players are assigned values: .5, 1.0, 1.5, 2.0, 2.5, 3.0, 3.5.

Hey, Slow Eddie, do women play?

Yeah, Spokes, they do. In the ongoing spirit of inclusion and fairness, women and those over 45 years old get a .5 reduction in their classifications.

So someone could potentially be a zero? Seems insulting to me.

It's a classification number, Ableman, not a character assessment. May I continue?

Sure, but stop leaving stuff out.

Each team must start four players and is allowed a maximum of 8.0 total points on the floor at a time, guaranteeing lower functioning and mid-functioning players plenty of playing time.[15] This turned out to be genius because low-pointers, as they are called, not only get to play but they are also critical to the strategy of every team. Most low-pointers start out being mid-pointer wannabes. I sure did. I wanted to be a scorer, the go-to guy like I was when we played recreational basketball before my injury. But some learn sooner rather than later that that is not going to happen. In Murderball low-pointers are primarily blockers—like linemen in football, without the bulk—and defenders. Once that reality sets in, low-pointers settle in to playing their role and they and their teams get that much better.

---

15 For example: (3.5 + 2.0 + 2.0 + .5 = 8) (3.0 + 2.5 + 1.5 + 1.0 = 8) (3.0 + 3.0 + 1.0 + 1.0 = 8). Any combination adding up to 8 is acceptable. Teams can have less than 8 points, not more.

Plus, Fast Eddie, they are the smartest.

What, because we were low-pointers ourselves?

No, because they're the smartest. They have to be. Low function means physically slower and less agile than high function. We make a mistake, too late, not like those showboat high-pointers who can screw-up and still make a play.

So, that makes low-pointers smarter?

Damn right. We're not prima donnas, either, but we make those primas look good. Remember that song we used to sing at practice?

Which?

"High Pointers Got No Reason To Live," sung to Randy Newman's insulting, tongue-in-cheek tune "Short People."

Seriously?

Well, they don't!

I first saw an exhibition in 1989. The Tampa Generals were an up-and-coming team that just a few years later would be a powerhouse in US quad rugby. I thought the idea of banging chairs together would be boring and senseless, like so many other so-called wheelchair sports. Basketball sucks for quads because most mid to low functioning quads can't get the ball to the hoop. Bowling was a joke for low-functioning quads: A ramp was placed on the bowling alley and the ball rested on the top of the ramp. The quad then pushed the ball onto the ramp and it would wobble its way down to the pins and feebly knock a few over. Yipee! It sucked. Most sports back then merely feigned competition; quads never really competed. Quad rugby changed all that. I knew the minute I saw those Tampa athletes in action that quad rugby was different. It changed everything. It was fast. Hard-hitting. Intense. Strategic. And most of all for me, it was real competition, no quarter asked for—none given.

I got home and made some calls and we formed a team: Dale, Monty, Joe, and me. The name: Sudden Impact. Our coach was Don Dawkins and our equipment man was Tom Kruse who owned a local medical supply store and later invented the Hoveround power wheelchair. Kruse scrounged up some old everyday chairs for us to play in. We practiced outdoors on a local grade school court. We didn't know shit. We couldn't do much of anything. Passing, catching and picking up the ball were even a challenge. It was frustrating, but we stayed with it because we wanted to play. Fortunately, Tampa had a very organized program with a great coach so we went up there to get the basics. They were light years ahead of us, so we thankfully learned a lot from the Tampa Generals and they kicked our asses for many years afterward as a "you're welcome."

We were classified. I was a 1.0. Joe a 1.0. Dale and Monty were both 2.0s and that's basically how we played for three or four years— with 6 points on the floor—2 shy of the maximum. Monty quit after a couple of years because he was tired of losing. We lost every game for the first few years.

You guys sucked.

We never had that high functioning player, Ableman.

We needed a 3.0 or 3.5 value player, big dogs we called them. Big dogs turned poor teams into good teams. We ran through quite a few guys, and when Nick (from the opening story) joined the team we were able to put 7 points on the court because Scott, a new player who replace Monty, and Nick were both classed as 2.0s. And we actually began to win a few games. Then Patrick showed up—our big dog arrived in the mid-nineties, a 3.0, and we started getting better and winning more games. We went from being dead last in the National rankings to the Top 20 in a couple of years.

We went through many name changes.

You were whores!

That's not true, Spokes. We were corporately aware.

Ok, Euphemistic Eddie: Sudden Impact, Healthsouth, Sarasota Riptide, Suncoast Lightning, Hoveround Lightning, Hoveround Gunners. You guys changed names like I change channels.

It was tough funding a team. We traveled all over the country and Canada to get to tournaments so we needed money. Plus, we needed equipment, rugby chairs, wheels, spoke guards, etc. We were lucky to have had the best equipment man of all time (and everything else from beer-runner to quad valet): Don Shapiro. He replaced Kruse in the '90s and was with us until the team disbanded.

Something more about Tom Kruse: Tom was a physical and financial supporter of the rugby team when he had practically nothing, and he was a loyal supporter after the Hoveround Corporation became a major success. From start to finish, through thick and thin, he supported the team and its players. For that, a special thank you from all the players who benefited from his generosity. Personally, I invested half of my entire savings to become a principle in Hoveround. My $10,000 bought me just a small percentage. The company sold in 1998 and the proceeds provided the base for our retirement. For that, too, I will always be grateful to Tom.

We also, in 2001, had Joe come on board as a player/coach. Remember him, the *Murderball* movie villain? We learned a ton from Joe. He was a great practice-coach, but as game-coach he had a yell-and-scream type intensity that surfaced now and then, but that wasn't who we were as a team. Although we were grateful and liked Joe personally, as a player/coach he was simply too much and had to go. The next year I took over coaching.

In 2003, after years of building and tough going, we played for the Division 1 National Championship in Phoenix; finishing second to the five-in-a-row champs Lakeshore Demolition from Birmingham, Alabama. We came up short, but we never finished out of the Top 5 after that until the team folded in 2009. We were even ranked Number 1 for about four months.

Twenty years! We had a great run and a great bunch of guys, and I tip my hat to every single quad that rolled a wheel playing Murderball for the Sarasota team. All told, it was probably thirty or forty guys and one girl, Lisa. Sorry to say I don't remember all the names because some players didn't stay around too long. So here goes: Monty, Dale, Joe M, Dick, Nick P, Jose, Serge, Justin, Pat, Joel, Rick, Dave W, DJ, Ross, Jairo, Joe S, Mike, Nick S, Lee, Scott, Mac, Carlos, Don, David, Bill, Mark C, Dave H, Aaron, Mark R, Ed, Russ, Marvin, Barry—Volunteers: Gary, Bill Z, Billy, Joey, Michael, Tom, Erik, Shane, Kim, Donald.

I played for over thirteen years and coached for six-plus. All during that time I also managed the team. In those early years, we were not very good. We didn't have the firepower, but we always had the desire.

We soon discovered that we were not alone in what Spokes refers to as our suckiness. Most teams were not in the upper tier. At any one time there were forty to fifty teams in the US with probably three to five really good teams. So each year the National Championships would be held and ten teams qualified, leaving the other thirty or forty on the outside looking in. I got involved with the workings of the United States Quad Rugby Association to change that. In 1995, we held the first Division 2 Tournament—The Sarasota Smash—and it grew into a 10-team tournament. The Smash's popularity prompted other teams to do the same and in 2000 the first official USQRA Division 2 tournament was held in Warm Springs, Georgia. Since then, 16 teams qualify for Nationals each year: Eight in Division 1 and eight in Division 2, keeping alive the spirit of inclusion in our sport.

I decided, especially after my SCIL debacle had just ended, to invest my time in promoting and advocating the sport, the pride, and independent living in the USQRA, at first as a Regional Assistant Commissioner in 2000 and later a board Vice President and then as President where I served from 2006 to 2010. I partnered with our board members to try to put more butts in the seats, which was a tall order because in spite of its fast, hard-hitting appeal, Murderball *is* played using a wheelchair—a knee-jerk turn-off for mainstream fans. US National Championships are lucky if they attract 200 fans over and above family and friends of the players. Oddly, the Paralympics are different. The quad rugby matches in Australia reached almost rock-star status. Australians knew the US players by name as they traveled there after the games. The Aussie players were national heroes. US players were astounded: 10,000 plus fans in the seats was unheard of. Even in Athens, Beijing and London that attendance trend continued. But it never has translated to cheeks in the seats here at home. Perhaps it's the Olympic spirit itself, the competition between nations that drives attendance. Whatever the reason, we thought we could boost attendance. The movie *Murderball* gave the USQRA huge momentum and we wanted to capitalize on that. We redid the USQRA logo, the web site, and started a monthly newsletter called "The Full Court Press." I wrote the introduction to quadrugby.com that the USQRA is still using today:

> The United States Quad Rugby Association exists to provide opportunity, support, and structure for competitive wheelchair rugby to people with disabilities. We are here to help people get involved in the fastest growing wheelchair sport in the world.
>
> Quad Rugby and the USQRA have changed lives. There is story after story of people getting involved with the sport who have found, through peer interaction or just the raw desire to compete, the competitive outlet they hadn't felt since before their disability. Some, disabled from birth or childhood, may be feeling the competitive fire for the first time. Almost without exception, the positive influence of this challenging sport transfers into players' everyday lives. That positive power may be the best thing we can say about our association and our game.
>
> Smashing Stereotypes One Hit at a Time is the main message of our players and our sport. Quad rugby is a tough, give-no-quarter game. Our players' lives – their successes and trials on and off the court – are a continuous example of smashing stereotypes. The sport is about ability and competitive fire. It is testament to the spirit of our great athletes, their humanity, and the intensity of our game.

There are fiercely independent people who have disabilities. Contrary to so-called common knowledge, many, many quads take care of themselves 100%. Like playing the sport, the more function you have the easier it is to be physically independent. The less function you have the more work that is required, so it takes a toll on the body over the years—and as it is for everyone else, old age is really a bitch. There is another saying/question among those in the know that asks, "Did you notice how much better Jason looks since he got married?"

Spouses and significant others make a huge, huge difference in keeping a better eye on skin, eating better, and all the other things someone you love brings to the table. Some quads don't want any extra help. Me, I'm spoiled rotten.

So the rugby community does far more than get quads fit to play the game. It is a learning center for independence far greater then any rehab hospital or college. Again, just like the game, you get no slack, yet there is experience and empathy woven into the advice you do get. Peers are critical teachers, sometimes compassionate, sometimes not. Eating more easily might be as simple as someone showing you how to hold a fork better. And when quads get together sooner rather than later they'll be talking about bowel and bladder. The damnedest things come up and often you learn something. You may or may not need to learn it or even want to learn it, but you do. Quads may have invented the term TMI.

Quads also gain stamina by training for and playing Murderball.

Hoop, you could hardly push two minutes at the mall back in the day. Pathetic! I was embarrassed to be seen with you.

You are me, Ableman.

My point exactly...

Regardless, it certainly gave me conditioning that I still try to maintain. I push 1 ½ to 2 miles a day and try to keep my weight under control. For those who need power chairs, I say, without joking, more power to them. I'll probably need one myself one day, but for now, I push. I thank quad rugby for that and for my strength and ability to transfer in and out of my car, my bed, and my shower/commode chair.

It doesn't have to be sports, though. It can be art or engineering or teaching or whatever and wherever your passions lead, but it takes a special person to go it alone. I think peers are the best things that can happen to someone who is newly injured, and outside of sport there aren't many activities that bring people with disabilities together, especially for long periods of time. Plus, there is hope and promise in seeing success being played out right it front of you. It's powerful. It does what Independent Living and support groups are supposed to do: teach that life with a disability is not the end, but a beginning. The newly injured person at first might hate the idea or think like many, including me, Dawkins and Nick, that it's just a bunch of cripples throwing a ball around. Murderball alumni would strongly disagree "one hit at a time."

Below is a photo of the original team and our 2003 team that played for the Division I United States Quad Rugby National Championship.

Early Tournament, crouching in front my wife Cindy and Tom. Don far right and then R-L: Joe, Dan, Scott, Dick, me, Dale, Kim, Monty.

2003 Team wins Sectional Championship and finishes second in Division 1 USQRA Championships. Don and Bill holding the banner. Seated (L-R) me, DJ, Dave, Joel, Mark, Dale, Patrick, Jairo, Lee.

CHAPTER 12

THE REALITIES OF REHAB

Sorry, Spokes, you're going to have to sit this chapter out.

Sit it out? Again! I practically missed the whole sex chapter. Is this your idea of another bad pun?

No, I just need to tell this without interruption.

You can't do this without me.

I have to. It's just one chapter.

Oh, all right, I'm bored already and you haven't even started, but I'm a clam.

After a severe spinal cord injury (SCI), how does a person with a permanent, paralyzing disability get to where he or she doesn't see him or herself as a worthless piece of crap? That's what we've learned, isn't it—that people with disabilities are doomed to unhappiness? Like able-bodied life, the disability road is cluttered with casualties, with too many falling by the wayside. Who or what is most important in seeing that the journey doesn't end by rolling off a cliff or popping a bullet into one's head, or sitting like a fern in the corner of a room for the rest of your life? So who? That person? Family? Peers? Rehab? Of course it's all of those things, but the process starts in rehab. I think when someone newly injured enters a rehabilitation hospital they have no clue that they are still valuable human beings who will need plenty of help and understanding to reclaim that person and that reality.

Rehab is the critical start to getting reattached to one's humanity and self-esteem. Newly injured persons need adequate time in rehab to initiate the process. With complications, I spent four-plus months in a rehab hospital—maybe that was too long, maybe not. But over the years that number has plummeted to where a newly injured person might spend as little as three weeks or less in rehab. What happened in the past thirty years to change that so dramatically? Managed care is what happened, one of the great oxymorons of our time. And very recently the Affordable Care Act (Obamacare) has happened as perhaps a start to righting this longtime wrong. Even now, though, big-money wants Obamacare repealed.

Before exploring the horrors that managed care has wrought upon people with disabilities, it's important to know that rehab hospitals don't work miracles. They work with people who have undergone dramatic physical and emotional change to be the best they can be out in the real world. The good hospitals will be the first to tell you that. But when the media latches on to a story that shows a patient walking out the doors of rehab facilities cured, it creates a problem for all those who couldn't walk out and for all those still inside who will never walk out. The news media love it, though, a juicy feature: the courageous story of the man or woman who fought back, battled the odds, and beat paralysis. But the good news story also creates the public perception that if you had only tried harder—like the "walking out hero"— you, too, could have walked out. It's not a sprained ankle. You don't "play your way through" a permanently damaged spinal cord.

My older brother Fred, may he rest in peace, came to see me in rehab. He always brought a rubber ball with him and told me if I'd just squeeze it over and over, I'd get my fingers moving again. The idea was that if I got those working, eventually I'd regain all my function. He would place the ball in my hand and it would roll off my palm. He would catch it and put it back, and say, "Just squeeze it." He hated seeing me paralyzed, and his face wrenched in pain at my predicament. The ball was his way of helping me, to give both he and me hope. I *did* try over and over, but the ball always rolled off. I would tell him each time that I couldn't squeeze the ball, but he kept placing it in the palm of my hand and saying, "Just squeeze it." Each time, it would roll off. After what seemed like 100 times, I screamed, "I can't squeeze that fucking ball!" I was immediately sorry, but Fred left pissed off and disappointed that I didn't try harder. It wasn't his fault; it's what he had learned—what we all have learned.

So, there are no heroes or miracles in rehab itself, just an injury that heals or doesn't heal. Some injured people work hard at rehab, some don't. "Walking out" does happen, and it is good public relations for the hospital, but it's not the norm or a snapshot of reality because most people with severe spinal-cord injures do not walk out of rehab hospitals; they roll out.

Rehab does, however, make a huge difference going forward, setting a solid foundation for building a new life on wheels. The better the rehab, the better the foundation. For me rehab felt a little like army basic training. I didn't like either the army or rehab (often hated them!) but they both helped me see that method, structure, and discipline were necessary in moving responsibly forward in my life. The physical therapists were like the drill instructors (far nicer) that pushed me to the max. Many times I wanted to say, "Screw you! I'm not doing this anymore." I never did, not to their faces anyway. Occupational therapists were just as insistent but they are more teachers than physical trainers: Getting dressed, brushing teeth—all the daily living stuff. Like the army, I wanted out, but it built character in spite of my dislike of the training and its institutional feel. Unlike the army, however, rehab was very difficult to leave because of the safety it provided.

Over the years since my release, a whole new paradigm of less and less insurance coverage took over in the US, and it slowly robbed newly injured people of that critical help and rehab foundation to build on.

Kurt was a hard-working independent contractor in Florida who could not afford health insurance. Heck, he was 31, healthy as a horse. What could go wrong?

Kurt was working trimming a tree in July 2012, fell twenty feet to the ground and broke his back and permanently injured his spinal cord. He was admitted into acute care, and, since he had no insurance coverage, Medicaid covered his hospital stay. Medicaid in Florida has followed a managed care path in systematically reducing benefits for catastrophic medical care. After Kurt was stabilized from his immediate, acute trauma, the hospital in week-two was already looking to discharge him. Kurt was absolutely in need of care but was getting pushed out the door because he couldn't pay. The fast track had started. Being a newly-injured paraplegic, Kurt needed a rehab hospital but was having a hard time finding a facility that would accept him with Medicaid coverage. "Medicaid beds," they call them. The acute care hospital was giving discharge deadlines so Kurt and his family were freaking out. After a major scramble by him and his family, a rehab facility was found. The only catch was that Florida Medicaid would only pay for three weeks of rehab for Kurt. Two months is probably what he needed.

How did Kurt cope? I tried to help him and did a little, as did his family and friends, but each injury is different. He also had Google and YouTube. Imagine, Kurt's body had just suffered a permanent, life threatening spinal-cord injury and his entire system was adjusting to the shock and trauma: Kidneys, bladder, bowel, muscles, lungs, heart—not to mention his psyche. And he gets three weeks of rehab, friends, family, Google, and YouTube to recover, learn, adjust, and face the world. That is as cruel as torture! But it's that quiet, nasty, distant torture that happens when corporate decision-makers assemble behind closed doors months and years earlier and make decisions about things like insurance coverage. They plant strategic exclusions, like little fine print pain-bombs, in individual and group policies to drastically reduce or eliminate coverage, and when people need that coverage everything blows up in their and their family's faces. The bombers have long since marched off to the bank with impunity to quietly and happily cash their checks for saving the company billions of dollars. Meanwhile, the Kurts of the world sit at home, or in a nursing facility, jerking with muscle spasms, fighting diarrhea and a 103° fever from a urinary tract infection—not knowing where to turn. Waterboarding would be far more humane.

Kurt somehow gutted it out and he is progressing, but what happens to someone without family and his kind of wherewithal to seek out and discern what is a good or bad course of action? Rehab is where that source of specialized, hands-on professional care should come from, not Google.

There is a societal underbelly to severe injury and disease that some people believe about disability, and that is: They had it coming. We've all heard the expression, "I wonder what he (or she) did to deserve that"? Too often people with disabilities are seen this way. It's biblical. Job's friends thought Job had committed a great sin and deserved his great suffering, which, as the story goes, he did nothing of the sort. We all know life can be inexplicably unfair—that all sorts of bad things happen to both good and bad people. In any case, if God saw fit to paralyze someone as punishment for bad, stupid, or despicable behavior the streets would have more gimps rolling around than cars. The blanket "he had it coming" thinking is both insulting and stupid at the same time.

We all know that it's always about the money. Spinal cord injuries are in the same "catastrophic" coverage category as traumatic brain injury (TBI), but TBIs are 200 times greater[16] than SCIs. So SCIs were lumped in with TBIs when it came to catastrophic insurance, and were hit with the same coverage exclusions as the bigger-dollar TBIs. The authors of the drastic reduction of catastrophic insurance coverage over the past thirty years don't care about the person; they care about the money. The shadowy perception out there in mainstream society that the injured person "had it coming" certainly didn't help put a stop to the coverage cuts.

Ironically and dismally, the injured person desperately needs money via insurance coverage for care. That road has turned into a one-way street leading away from those who need catastrophic coverage and the critical care it provides. It then becomes a dead-end street for the newly injured, leaving them no way to facilitate proper recovery. And *that* is the immoral consequence of sending newly brain and spinal-cord-injured people back into society neither medically nor emotionally prepared. It is a moral crime.

I had the pleasure recently of speaking to Kenny Hosack, Director of Provider Relations, from Craig Hospital in Denver, CO. Craig was just ranked #1 Rehab Hospital by the American Nursing Association NDNQI in February 2014 for the third year out of the last four. I told Hosack Kurt's story. He was sad to hear that Kurt did not have insurance, and was unaware of Florida's Medicaid restriction on length of stay. He pointed out that Colorado uses "medical necessity" as the criterion for length of stay. Each state has different Medicaid benefits, he said. Hosack also sent me a Craig report that was just as alarming as

---

16 http://www.cdc.gov/traumaticbraininjury/severe.html

Kurt's story. It's possible that the lousy coverage Kurt had under Florida Medicaid might have been better than what Kurt could have bought privately. Here is the telling part of that 2011 report (bolding is mine):

Unfortunately, most people these days do not have adequate rehabilitation coverage, either in their individual policies, or in their employer group policies. **Over the last three decades in the marketplace the transition from an indemnity insurance model to various managed care health plan products has significantly reduced or eliminated adequate rehabilitation coverage from most common health plans.** The original principal of "insurance" – to protect people in the event of major losses – has been reversed and health plans now cover relatively minor health care encounters, but not serious injuries. Sadly, individuals and employers typically don't realize the severe limits of their inpatient and outpatient benefits until a catastrophic injury occurs.

And:

Unless employers are well educated about how to read the fine print in their policies, they may renew a policy that eliminates benefits they never intended to eliminate.

Craig has alarming case studies supporting their statement. Individuals who were uninformed about changes to, or the elimination of, their catastrophic insurance coverage were screwed, especially if they didn't qualify for Medicaid. Then along came Obamacare.

The 2010 Affordable Care Act (ACA) mandates rehabilitation, habilitation, and durable medical equipment coverage in 2014 for those who signed up, but leaves many of the details up to the individual states. The mandate is excellent for consumers, not so good for insurers. The insurance companies deplore the ACA mandate because it undoes all the hard, fine-print work insurers did gutting and eliminating catastrophic coverage over the years, especially if existing consumers get wise and start demanding rehab coverage themselves in their private and group policies. Follow the money: With an educated guesstimate of 12,000 spinal-cord injuries a year and an average of 60 rehab days at $3000 per day—that is $2.16 billion a year. Traumatic brain injuries (TBIs) in 2010 were estimated to cost $76.5 billion.[17] Insurance companies saved billions over thirty years. So who paid? Well, we all did: Individuals who didn't get the care they needed; taxpayers through Medicaid and other government assistance; and the hospitals themselves. We all paid the tab, except the insurance companies, of course. They saved while you and I paid, as is the case with pre-existing conditions and countless other exclusions, so when the ACA said "no more" to all of that, it created billions of reasons for insurance companies to detest and want to repeal Obamacare.

The ACA also has embraced a new kid in town: Accountable Care Organization (ACO). This is basically a network of actual healthcare providers that is similar to managed care in that you get penalized outside the ACO network. The jury is still out as to whether this is a good overall healthcare delivery method. For rehab it doesn't look promising. ACOs limit choice outside the closed network, and there are already too few excellent choices in the US.

According to Hosack, there are only a handful of specialized SCI and TBI rehabilitation hospitals in the U.S., and only a small percentage of patients are able to get to the specialty hospitals. General rehab centers simply cannot offer the services and patient outcomes of specialty centers. For example, most general rehab hospitals have eliminated therapeutic recreational therapist (TR) from their treatment facilities completely. TRs are the professionals, like Don Dawkins, who take newly-injured people out to restaurants, riding buses, to sporting events, etc., to help them reintegrate, navigate, and cope in the world. TRs can be game changers, like Dawkins did in helping Nick in

17 http://www.cdc.gov/traumaticbraininjury/severe.html

the Murderball chapter. That profession is practically gone except in better hospitals like Craig. But if the cuts in coverage continue, TR as a professional occupation and the vital treatment it provides will die and be forgotten.

For those who love the bottom line: good rehab is good business. The return on investment (ROI) is awesome. There is a direct correlation between high quality rehab to a greater percentage of independence, school/employment, and quality-of-life outcomes. For example, Craig has a 36% return to work/school percentage for a C-5 to C-8 quad who has a 90-day average inpatient stay. The national average is around 17%. In every category, Craig scores better than the national average. This means that excellent rehab saves taxpayers billions over the years because people with spinal-cord and brain injury are better prepared to become working taxpayers again when they receive top notch rehab. The model for rehab care is right there for everyone to follow; the outcomes speak for themselves; better rehab is better for the economy and more importantly it is better for the person.

Managed care has done its own bottom-line work well by providing limited coverage or eliminating it completely over the years. The result: Unspoken hardship and private suffering being endured by injured people nationwide. For those without proper rehab, that suffering goes on hour after hour, day after day, year after year. Hidden from us is that private hell. Hidden from us is the fact that inadequate rehabilitation services usually result in increased medical complications, which adds more pain for the person, and it ultimately cost far more to resolve long-term than the tab for rehabilitation itself. Both privately and governmentally, it really is "pay now" so we're not all paying later. Insurers don't pay now, and certainly won't pay later, especially if Obamacare is repealed.

The real miracle is that facilities like Craig have found ways to maintain their services as the coverage dollars have been siphoned away nationwide by lawmakers and managed care. I know this won't reach too many managed-care or budget-cutting ears, but providing catastrophic coverage for those who need it is **the right thing to do.**

All right, Hooper, you said be quiet, but these numbers and stats are boring the shit out of me. Besides, I don't trust insurance companies as far as I can sprint.

You don't need to, Spokes, this is about rehab and the moral need for it.

Oh, yeah, what about care? Who's caring for those who need it after rehab? No, the better question is who cares <u>about</u> those who need the help?

You're right, Spokes, it is a much deeper well. We've heard the saying, "It takes a village" to raise a child. So, too, does it take a village to help one recover from a life-changing disability. Rehab doesn't stop at the hospital exit door; it's a lifelong process.

No, it never stops if you're moving forward. What about that discussion you had with Irving Zola?

I had the pleasure of speaking with Zola before he died in 1994. Professor Zola taught at Brandeis University and he was an internationally known activist and writer in the fields of medical sociology and disability rights. He was a founding member of the Society of Disability Studies and the first editor of Disability Studies Quarterly. He was also a founding member and counselor at the Boston Self-Help Center.[18]

---

18 http://www.zolacenter.org/10/

Here are parts of that conversation that ring as true today as they did then:

HOOPER: In rehab we are advised to push ourselves to the maximum of our physical capabilities, but we're never given any limits. How do we know what is too much?

ZOLA: How do we know the doctors don't tell us to push too much all the time? It's too often an either/or situation in our rehabilitation. It's sort of been a philosophy of "use it or lose it." It's a reality that if you don't exercise, in the most general sense, that there may be some physiological risks. But it's a reality that we could have a choice about. By using a power wheelchair, for example, rather than propelling yourself, you could expand the nature of your life by being able to go an extra 900 or 1200 yards. You may not become as strong or get as much exercise; but one of the issues of choice has to be the ability to take certain risks and make certain trade-offs.

HOOPER: When we go through rehab, we are naive and introspective. We're in no shape to make demands on anyone; we are at the mercy of the professionals. Whose responsibility is it to see that we are given the information so that we can make these choices?

ZOLA: We may have to push for legislation. That's what the women had to do. Short of that unlikely remedy, we may require varying advocacy groups that are resident within hospitals and other health care institutions. We have seen bits and pieces of that: a booklet that tells you your rights as a patient; a phone number that you can call. I would suggest a spinal cord injury service (obviously, not in the most acute stages) be available with anything from informational booklets to the possibility of seeing certain organizations like Independent Living Centers.

HOOPER: To me the key word in real independence is control. Let's try to define independence as it relates to disability.

ZOLA: Control means decision-making. It means that regardless of the consequences (unless it's an extremely technical procedure), the individual on whom that procedure is being done—or where decisions are being made about their life—they have to be at the center of that decision. Disability, just by definition, makes us more dependent than people with acute illness, for example. We have been more physically dependent for a long period of time without any great physical recovery.

HOOPER: Our society is used to people going in with an ailment or illness, getting better and coming out—or going in and dying.

ZOLA: That's right. We are already one down if you will, from that particular perspective. Now, what is temporary for people with an acute illness becomes permanent for those of us with a chronic condition.

HOOPER: In a hospital atmosphere: they strip you down naked, both literally and dignity-wise. And it seems to me that many people with disabilities cannot get their clothes back on.

ZOLA: That's a good metaphor. This kind of stripping process goes on for patients in all kinds of institutions—particularly long term ones—and I think that stripping is what happens in the beginning.

HOOPER: Leaving rehab can be freaky. I was deathly afraid to go anywhere without Cindy. And when she was gone, I worried something would happen that I couldn't control. When I finally went out on my own—took a chance—my state of mind and hers were reborn. Do you see this kind of dependence in other people with disabilities?

ZOLA: Oh, sure. But even though we can experience this on the most personal level, deep down, the dilemma is social. One of the reasons you get into that position is that it is so difficult at this time to get one or two people in whom you can trust to respond to your needs. Indeed, you get afraid to lose them, so much so that you become more dependent on them, and probably *give in* to the needs you really want some of the time. You curb yourself. If we had anything from a national to local registry, if it were recognized as a general service, if it were accepted as a kind of occupation, which people could go into and go out of, then the pool of people that we could turn to would be so great that we wouldn't be constantly concerned about losing that one person—even if it is one we love.

HOOPER: Isn't it reasonable for someone to have a wife, a significant other, a mother, a father, or whoever, and a separate personal care attendant? Some people are simply not cut out to do this kind of work.

ZOLA: Absolutely. Home health care.

HOOPER: So, you're the boss; you should trust that person to be dependable, and you must do the same in return; you should be comfortable with the person you choose; that person should not slough off on your needs; and, you both treat it like a service not a favor, right?

ZOLA: The best model is out at Berkeley.[19] They treat it like a professional occupation. (Note: It's still there in 2015.) They have really large training sessions for anyone who could use a personal care attendant, and they have a network, which brings the two together.

HOOPER: This is also critical for those already physically independent as that can change more suddenly when you already have a

---

19 http://www.cilberkeley.org/personal-attendant-referrals/

disability. Shoulders go out. Things change as we age. It would liberate the person by taking away that fear.

ZOLA: Exactly. There is a shortage of people to do these personal care tasks, so we, in our high-tech society, have turned to other means: robots and monkeys. Every time, in our society, we go for the technological "fix" and what is the short-term solution ultimately becomes the long-term way of dealing with it. By replacing human needs—that is, the nature of care: touching, being present, etc.—we cannot help but contribute to the long-term isolation and the objectification of the individual. It doesn't mean there is no place for robots or animals, all right?

HOOPER: Yeah. I was thinking monkeys would be okay like guide dogs are for blind people.

ZOLA: That's right. Companion dogs and guide dogs have a particular function. You can have a human relationship, but you use that guide dog to enable you to get around.

HOOPER: You testified as an expert witness in a personal injury suit recently and a $4 million verdict was won. You didn't present your testimony in the typical "vegetable," "basket case" mold used in all these cases, which has to leave a plaintiff feeling worthless. You talked about the financial burdens of disability, about civil rights being lost because of an inaccessible society, and what it's really like out in the world for someone with a disability. How did the people in the courtroom react to this?

ZOLA: There was a good deal of surprise, and for a certain segment of the group there was a real recognition of what the hell I was talking about. This trial was held in Washington D.C. The plaintiff and the defendant were white, as were the lawyers, the expert witness, and the judge. But the jury was all black. Now, when I turned to the jury and started to describe in detail—quite honestly, consciously—of what it was like to be a second-class citizen, and discussed the real burdens of disability: high-priced equipment and housing; inaccessible restaurants, theaters, transportation, housing; job discrimination; segregation. That jury knew what the hell I was talking about. They may not have read about the social construction of disability, but they knew how society could make someone feel: second-class and worthless—by going through back entrances, secondary facilities—segregated, and poor. I then told the jurors that the plaintiff needed money for equality.

HOOPER: Would a white jury have reacted the same way?

ZOLA: Probably not as dramatically, but I think a white jury would have been able to hear the issues. If I may add a personal footnote: We labor in the vineyards, so to speak, and we are taking little steps, and I've got to tell you that trial had to be one of the greatest personal satisfactions I have ever been part of.[20]

- end of discussion

In light of the typically debasing "vegetable" and "fate worse than death" arguments presented in our courts, Zola's portrayal had to enrich this disabled man's state of mind. What's more, it left him with something even a billion dollars could never have bought: his dignity.

With baby boomers aging, there is more demand for care, and home care is becoming more and more available. Companies like www.care.com offer services to adults like bathing and dressing. I

---

20 A footnote of my own: Outside my family and friends, two of my best personal satisfactions were talking—ever so briefly—to Irving Zola and Ed Roberts. I feel so blessed and privileged to have spoken with them both.

know nothing of their scope or quality of service, but the fact that they are thriving is proof of the need and demand for care.

The reality in this great country is that money rules. At every level the battle for money is waged. Managed care—along with Wall Street, Washington D.C., and state legislators—have professionals working day and night to simply get more money and make more cuts, usually to those who can least resist. Will the axe-wielders ever stop and look at the person and his or her suffering? I don't think they will; they serve the god of cash. The largest reality for rehab may have nothing to do with all the great work rehab does or doesn't do, but rather can it be saved from the cold, cost-cutting axe? Or will that coverage be slashed into something that provides nothing resembling real, proven rehab care—beaten to death at the altar of greed?

If ever a nation needed universal healthcare, it is we.

CHAPTER 13

ODDS AND LOOSE ENDS

I. Paralyzing Language

"The Midwest has been crippled by blinding snow and gale-force winds. Air traffic at Chicago's O'Hare Field is completely paralyzed."

"Good evening. This is the CBS Evening News with Scott Pelly."

"Wait a second, Scotty," Spokes Ableman interrupts. And, like something out of a Sci Fi novel, Pelly can hear and converse with Spokes on national television, but neither he nor CBS engineers can tune Spokes out.

"Scotty? Who's calling me Scotty? Who is this?! Just a moment, ladies and gentlemen, someone has obviously hacked his way into our transmission," Pelly tells viewers.

"Scott, this is Spokes Ableman. I've been listening to your continual use of disability to personify natural disasters, crop failures, stock declines—virtually everything related to failure. And we have to talk."

"No we don't, Mr. Ableman."

"Call me Spokes. And yes we do. Don't you see any of this language as offensive?"

"No," Pelly replies cautiously. "Are you, ah, paralyzed, Mr. Ableman?"

"It's Spokes. And yes Scott I am paralyzed, and I'm no freaking disaster. Between you and those five lunkheads on *60 Minutes*, disability has been taken on a stereotype roller-coaster ride from beating all odds to tear-jerk tragedy."

"Mr. Ableman, are you confined to a wheelchair, an invalid?"

"You mean like in-valid as in not valid? Look, Scott, it's Spokes, or Ableman if you get pissed off in the next couple of minutes. No, I'm not an invalid or confined to a wheelchair. I use it. Do you see bars or walls around any of the wheelchairs that roll around Manhattan?

"What's that suppose to mean?" Pelly asks. Then to the audience: "We're working on this problem, ladies and gentlemen.

"I mean, Scott, that my wheelchair was not something I got for committing a crime. I use it, period. Understand?"

"Yes, I think so. You're wheelchair-bound?"

"Jesus Christ, Scott, I'll be New York bound to staple your tie to your news desk if you can't get this straight. I'm not "confined," nor am I "bound," "shackled,' 'handcuffed," 'hogtied'—nothin'. I use the chair. Got it?"

"Okay, okay, I understand. Now, will you please return control of our newscast, Mr. Ableman?"

"Sure, Scott. Are you going to watch that 'loaded' language you use—the language that puts down people with disabilities?"

"Yes. NOW, please!"

"No 'lame duck' references, Scott?"

"No. Come on!

"Ok then, it's back to you, Scott. David and Brian are next. Fox is hopeless. So good evening to you."

"We're sorry, ladies and gentlemen, our transmission was somehow pirated by someone calling himself Spokes Ableman. Our broadcast was temporarily disabled ... "

"Hello, Scotty. This is Spokes, again."

The above satire came from listening to the evening news the other night and hearing, for what seemed like the millionth time, disability being used as a negative metaphor. The language is anchored in our society. Even though I thoroughly understand the importance of words and the impact they have on us, I almost didn't think a section on language would be necessary. The book, I thought, would make clear how one needs to characterize one's self. That broadcast demonstrated how wrong I was. I started listening again for offensive words rather than just letting them roll off my back. I was shocked that these clichés never seem to lose their allure.

Plus, quite recently a friend of mine objected rather vigorously to my use of "disabled person" even "disabled," to describe him and his disability. "Disabled implies unable. I am not unable," he said, insulted by my usage. We argued for a short time, until we discovered that we were both saying pretty much the same thing, just using different words.

This is also what prompted me to explain my usage of "disabled person" in the Introduction. When using "disabled," I use it not to say that the individual person is unable or less than a person—quite the contrary. Before going any further, I think it's important to repeat one last time that we are all simply people, some of us happen to have disabilities.

It then occurred to me that the semantics of how we are described and how we describe ourselves need more exploration. Insulting words can get tossed around freely if people with disabilities smile and nod in apparent agreement, when deep down they are more than a little offended.

Certain words and phrases will not suit everyone, but they can be examined to see how they are being used—to find out why they are taken with such indignation. Thus far, most of my anger has been directed at the media and its ignorant opinions (to be discussed later), but it seems many of disability's own words and phrases are dredging up some anger of their own.

The disability community has yet to come up with a go-to word, uniting the perceptions and feelings of "otherness" we share in our physical being. I've tried; it's a real brain twister. What do blind people, deaf people, paralyzed people, and others have in common for group identification purposes besides disability itself? Not much. So coming up with a catchall name is no mean task.

There are some obvious problems with "disabled person" and "handicapped person," regardless of my good intentions. It does, after all, say your personage is somehow disabled. Still, I use "disabled person" here and there because so far it has proven to be the best of a barrel full of rotten-apple words. And at least we put disability and the person together, and do not, as has often been done, make the person and the disability the same.

We see "the disabled" and "the handicapped" used over and over again. For reasons unclear, yet no less annoying to me, "the handicapped" has associated with it a kind of loathsome finger pointing, perhaps from phrases like "Hire The Handicapped." Or my favorite "Handicapped Parking." I do not have a cap on my handy, yet I use the word myself to show my disdain. When I say it, I twist each syllable with a certain emphasis: HON - DEE -COPPED.

To my ears, however, "the disabled" isn't quite as insulting. It has been argued that "the disabled" is a perfectly good usage of an adjective as a noun, like the rich, the poor, the young, etc. That makes sense, but when I get tempted toward such usage, because of the nagging repetition of "disabled person" or the sometimes unmanageable "person with a disability," I think of headlines in newspapers, and I quickly look for another way to state my meaning.

Some people would rather be called a "cripple" straight out. Nancy Mairs, for example, in her fine essay, "On Being A Cripple," says she prefers it. She writes: "Whatever you call me, I remain crippled. But I don't care what you call me, so long as it isn't differently abled, which strikes me as pure verbal garbage designed, by its ability to describe anyone, to describe no one." Mairs feels that "cripple" cuts right to the heart of her multiple sclerosis, and one can only respect her right to call herself whatever she likes. But for me, "cripple" is a harsh word with its "K"-sound snapping in my ears like a dried twig. It's also the "whispered word" used frequently by society, even though most consider "cripple" to be pejorative. And, like most disability words, it is hardly descriptive of a blind or deaf person. So, while "cripple" is a defiant word, it carries with it too much negative baggage to be effective as disability's liberating signature. And let's not forget that the news media everywhere love "cripple" as their favorite headline or lead-in to depict devastation.

Blacks took a word that was used against them and turned it into "black is beautiful." It's amazing to think that slurs like "black-assed nigger" and "black bastard" helped spawn "black" as a word both Blacks and society came to accept. But Blacks had the same thing in common: the color of their skin. Still, it took them hundreds of years of struggling to find the pride to call themselves something that was mutually acceptable for both them and society.

Homosexuals managed to take "gay," which until 40 years ago meant happy, and turned it into the socially accepted way of referring to themselves. What a brilliant use of a word!

Women stuffed bitch right back down our throats. Everyone is calling everyone a "biatch" these days. The usages have ever so slightly defused the nasty impact of bitch. Men call men bitches. For women, I would imagine that bitch is nothing like being called a "cunt," perhaps the most insulting word in the English language. I wouldn't, however, recommend looking seriously at a woman and saying, "You are such a bitch."

Disability, however, doesn't have such a history of open bigotry. We've pretty much been discussed in whispers or in corners and closets. Few people had the audacity to call us cripples, freaks or monsters (to our faces, that is), so we, supposedly, had nothing to take offense at. But we weren't listening closely enough. If so, we would have heard "cripple" spoken when we were presumed not listening, much like "nigger", "faggot" and "cunt" were and are used by prejudicial members of society when Blacks, Gays and women are out of earshot. It still goes on. But those words would never see a headline in a newspaper or lead-in to a TV broadcast.

There is still a distinction, though, in that "nigger", "faggot" and "cunt" are generally spoken out of some ignorant hatred, and "cripple" is still uttered out of some ignorant pity. It's difficult to show anger toward someone who displays the weight of his/her good intentions toward you like an albatross. Nevertheless, if what we feel is anger, we need to say so—at the very least we should say that we don't like it, not unkindly, but seriously tell the person that it offends you.

It's not as though people aren't trying to find a name that somehow captures the message of the disability movement into a tightly wrapped package. "Physically challenged" is being used, but, when you think about it, "physically challenged" is a rather silly euphemism: your body has issued a challenge, respond or be, what, defeated and be forever "physically unchallenged"? Given only two choices, I'd choose "cripple," with all its nastiness, over "physically challenged" every time.

Next up is what must be the most ridiculous word of the lot: "handi-capable." When I first read this superfluous hyphenation, I misread it as "handicap-able," which takes on a slightly more interesting meaning. I can't see the disability community dancing to the beat of this euphemistic intrusion.

"Quad," "para," "gimp," and "crip" are all insider words. One does not hear these words too often in mainstream conversation. When someone, usually a peer, asks if I'm a "quad," what he's asking is, "Do you have quadriplegia?" Because of the clinical awkwardness of the longer names, injured persons decided (who knows when?) to abbreviate and become "paras" and "quads." Spoken among those people with such disabilities, it's perfectly fine, but there is harm in thinking that "quad" or "para" is the predominant factor in what makes someone a person. And it can happen. Irving Zola in Chapter Twelve voiced a great deal of concern over this during our conversation. He said, "What I struggle against—in the most concrete way—is nouns, because nouns make us and the disability the same."

This is precisely why the media cranks out the same metaphors ad nauseam that I introduced at the beginning of this chapter. It makes disability and disaster the same.

"Gimp" and "Crip," like most of the "in" words, don't take into account all of the disability community. Both words denote physical mobility difficulties. "Gimp" has been around a long time. I remember my grandfather saying, "It's tough getting around on this gimpy leg." I've used "gimp" more and more over the years because it neither immediately offends nor nauseates, and it doesn't shackle me to being automatically perceived as a victim. It doesn't make the disability and the person one. That's why you'll never see the headline: MIDWEST GIMPED BY WINTER STORM.

"Crip" is, of course, short for "cripple." It doesn't sound quite as bad, though. Unfortunately, neither does it sound very good. "Crip" carries all the baggage of "gimp," "quad," and "para" with "cripple" lurking one syllable away as its weighty etymon. Plus, there's a street gang in L.A. that has already laid claim to the word Crip. As far as I'm concerned, they can keep it.

Anything we with disabilities come up with must be better than how we're currently described in literature and the media. Here is the media's Big 6: "victim," "afflicted," "suffering," "courageous," "overcoming," and "inspirational" (with variations of each thereof). It would be difficult to read a story about someone disabled that doesn't have one of these tags—as if the label is a given. One day I expect to see a story start like this (if one hasn't already been written):

Jane Jones, an accident victim, afflicted and suffering since 2002, has overcome her paraplegia to graduate Harvard Law School. Her courageous efforts are inspirational to us all.

To reword the above story: "Good God! How could a 'cripple' do it"?

Most people, I think, could be persuaded to see the fallacy in using "afflicted," "suffering," and "courageous." Each is an opinion with absolutely no basis in fact. The above story assumes each as a natural product of disability when the graduate could easily have been as healthy as a marathon runner, and the biggest backstabbing, cowardly asshole to have ever attended law school. Also, Jane graduated with her disability; she didn't "overcome" it.

"Victim," like a ball and chain, carries with it all kinds of unnatural, negative weight. But many people, even disabled people, cannot see any harm in using "victim" to describe someone's disability. It has been argued that "victim" denotes a helplessness that comes from a deliberate act against one's person: a robbery victim, for example. Being hit by a car is usually indiscriminate. You are not targeted, but when taken in the strictest context of a singular event in her life, Jane Jones was a "victim," but must Jane lug around with her the lifelong sentence of this highly charged, negative word, becoming shackled and stigmatized with each turn of a phrase? Victims who fully recover are not victims their entire lives. Maybe that's why we continually read about people "confined to a wheelchair"; they're unjustly serving time in the media's innuendo penitentiary. And lest we forget, Jane's accident happened twelve years ago. She's a graduate from Harvard Law, not an accomplishment of someone who has lived her life as perpetual "victim."

This leads to the big one, "Inspirational." This word is used much like "courageous" is, but can be more easily defended. One might ask: Why, without enough good role models to go around, is it unreasonable to be inspired by someone who was severely injured and has just graduated from Harvard? That question evokes a question: What exactly is "inspirational"— her graduation or her paralysis? And: Why, when people need relief from the blue funk of world events, are people with disabilities the designated inspirators?

Presumed Innocent, Scott Turow's bestseller, has a scene that punctuates the idea of disability as a hope-giver. The character Lydia MacDougall is a successful woman prosecuting attorney, who is also a paraplegic. In part, here is how the narrator describes her:

> As the jurors get a couple of days to think about what it would be like to have their legs flapping around, loose as flags, as they listen to this woman, handsome, forceful, good-humored, absorb the wedding ring, the casual mention of her baby, observe the fact that she is—impossibly—normal, they are full of admiration and, as we all should be, hope.

We cannot, it seems to me, be "inspirational" when we're continually being portrayed as "impossibly—normal." MacDougall is presented as a well-adjusted human being, which makes me think Turow was trying to be complimentary—so why the editorial? It's assumed, that's why. Certainly, people with disabilities need heroes and good role models just like everyone else, but not the could-be-worse, look-what-the-brave-cripple-can-do depictions. We need far more role models, like Ed Roberts, Stevie Wonder and Stephen Hawkins[21] and countless others in the day-to-day world, who come out and inspire people with disabilities to be proud inside their own skin. Now that would truly be "inspirational"!

Disability's language is a muddle. With the loaded usage by the media, and with disabled people and outsiders searching for a name, is it any wonder that we have such a hodge-podge of words and jaded usages? I don't think we yet have the sense of total community that will make our choices clear in all matters—including an acceptable name. Many have tried very hard to break the restraints of the old attitudes, the old images, the old language, and the old influence. Women, Blacks, and Gays have only recently begun to loosen the knots that re-strained them for hundreds (thousands!) of years. We've just begun our fight. Until we get named and portrayed with some dignity, it seems like "disabled" is near to what "colored" was for Blacks 60 years ago: "Colored" was much better than "nigger," but not nearly as good as "Black" or Afro American. For me, "disabled" is better than "handi-capped" and far better than "cripple," but not nearly as good as... What?

II. Quarter For Your Thoughts

Happy Birthday Spokes!

Thanks, Hoop, 36-years-old last Wednesday. Man what a ride.

Hey, Ableman, how about tellin' one of those stories about how some folks are really good relating to people in wheel-chairs, and others, well, not so much?"

---

21 I plan to see *The Theory of Everything*. I'm not overly optimistic, but have an open mind.

You mean GWGs?

What's a GWG?

Good With Gimps, Hoop. Is there anything that you do know about this stuff?

Then I assume, Mister Know-it-all, the other side of that coin is Bad With Gimps?

Good thinking. Yeah, some BWG's are downright infuriating, Hooper. Others—God love 'em—are just hopelessly helpful. I've had people run to open a door for me and almost break their own necks in the process. Good intentions, bad with gimps.

Here's one that I didn't find too funny:

I'm in the mall, sitting outside a shoe store waiting for my wife. Now, Bunny's not exactly a shoe-aholic, but she's no slouch when it comes to slipping on a sandal or two. So, I'm sitting there for a good while.

Doing what?

Ah, daydreamin'—people watchin'. Anyway, I had just finished a cup of coffee and was holding the empty paper cup on the top of my leg. So, I'm sitting there thinking of God-knows-what when I hear this little "plunk" and the cup moves. I look inside the cup and there's George Washington starin' up at me.

What!? Whoa, someone tossed a folded-up buck in your cup?

No, a quarter! Can you believe it? Someone—I didn't see who— dropped a damned quarter into the cup and disappeared into the crowd.

Ha, ha, ha, ha, ha, oh my God, a quarter? What did you do?

Well, I took off in the direction I thought this rather frugal Good Samaritan went and yelled as loud as I could, "You forgot your pencil! You forgot your pencil! You forgot your pencil!"

You're kidding, right?

No way, but there was no guilty person turning around, just a bunch of stunned shoppers thinking I was the one who had issues.

Gee, I wonder why, Spokes?

You know, Hoop, this person was not only dissing me, but a skinflint to boot—a quarter, 25 cents! That's just cruel. What if I really was begging? What am I supposed to buy with a quarter, a bubble-gum ball to raise my blood sugar just above coma level?

Heck, Spokes, some of those bubble gum balls are fifty cents.

That's not the point, Hooper. My God! This person saw a wheelchair and immediately thought, "I must help this poor wretch somehow." Where he or she came up with the 25-cent-solution, I have no idea.

I know, Spokes, but you have to admit it's really funny.

No, not funny, Hooper, pathetic that someone sees "wheel-chair" and thinks "needy." Besides, don't these Bad With Gimps have any folding money with Ben Franklin's face on them?

III. Aisle Chairs

Spokes, do you remember the first time we encountered an aisle chair?

The dreaded aisle chair… Who could forget? Frightening!

To fully understand the indignities of an aisle chair it helps to know that wheelchair-users of the world suffer the same indignities as short people and small children: We can't see over clothing racks; we must stretch and strain to be seen and heard at a cash register; we get buried in a standing ovation, pledge of allegiances or any "please stand" activity. We are functionally short, and we can, if not careful, experience a psychological shortness too: an overwhelming feeling of being in a hole. Any large function can put you there. As long as everyone is seated, things are okay. But as people stand up and begin milling around, the distinct feeling of being in a hole can be created merely by me being in a wheelchair when everyone else standing. A wheelchair-user makes his/her own little hole in the crowd.

Wheelchair shortness—that feeling of getting lost in the sea of people—can become a thin thread separating how we are physically and how we feel emotionally. There's nothing wrong with being either short or disabled, but it's critical to stay out of the emotional hole. It siphons off our self-esteem like a licensed thief.

Hanging on to one's self-esteem and dignity can often be a full-time job because the challenges come in many forms, and not just in crowds. My wife Cindy and I decided to go on vacation by air. This was my first flight since becoming disabled, and we weren't taking any chances. We arrived at O'Hare Field three hours early. That's when I first learned about aisle chairs. The aisles in commercial aircrafts are too narrow to accommodate a regular wheelchair so aisle chairs must be used. I was informed that I should go to the gate and get a claim tag put on my everyday chair and then get into the aisle chair for boarding. Then my wheelchair would be taken down and put directly on the plane. Sounded good. That was before I saw the aisle chair

I swear, Hooper, you couldn't land a sparrow's ass on that thing.

Yeah, that's the first reaction. It must be like 12 inches wide. It looks like a dolly with a long narrow seat.

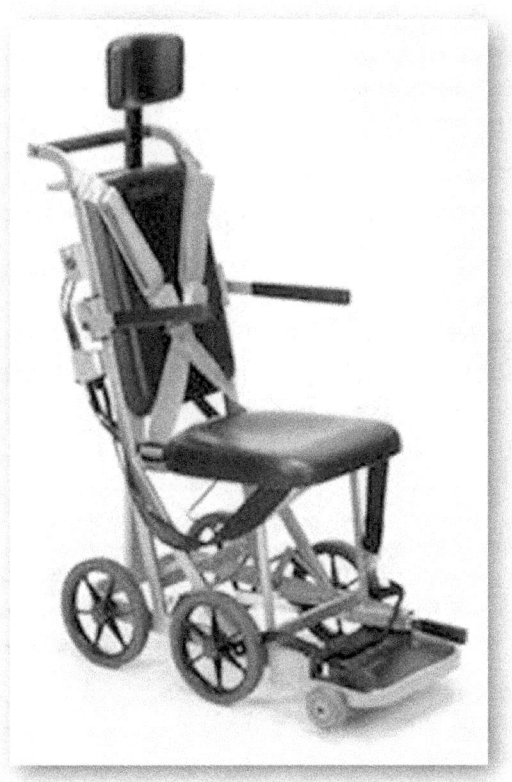

It freaked me out. And these airline people are telling us not to worry. As soon as I hear that, I'm worried! So, they push me down to the boarding door...

Yeah, Spokes, but they have no clue how to get me from my wheelchair into the aisle chair and then from there into my seat.

I know, right. If I transferred myself, it would be like trying to land my keister on a dime. Dicey.

Right, so they call for a guy (took him 10 minutes to get there) who could lift me up from behind and Cindy took my legs to make sure they didn't botch up the transfer. Meanwhile people are waiting to board. Gimps board first.

Yep, otherwise we'd be swallowed up in the boarding melee. Anyway, they get me in the aisle chair and then the strapping-in begins. By the time they're done, I looked like Hannibal Lecter without the plastic mask covering my face. Maybe they should have done the mask, too, because I was getting an intense urge to bite someone.

Onto the plane we go with my dignity checked at the gate along with my wheelchair. Smiles of, "Welcome on board" greeted me as we passed precariously down the aisle. It's hard to explain the feeling; you just suck it up and can't wait to be out of the thing.

Shit, Hoop, just then my leg pops off of the aisle chair and it starts banging into the armrests. The guy says, "Hold your arms and legs together." I say, "How? I'm bound up here like convict." So, they stop and put my foot back, and we make our way to the seat.

Meanwhile, Spokes, Bunny is scrambling around getting my cushion and the rest of our carry-on loaded into the overhead.

It was time to unchain Hannibal and deposit him in his seat. Well, the "don't worry" folks go to pick me up and I barely budge. It was like I weighed 250 pounds not 140. After a few more failed efforts with the aisle chair lurching about, it was discovered that the armrest on the aisle chair was not folded up and my hip and leg were caught under it. More bruises.

We finally got in the seat, Spokes, and the plane got loaded. Cindy had the window seat. As the plane was pulling away from the gate, she saw my wheelchair sitting out on the tarmac and yelled, "Stop the plane! Stop the plane! Stop the plane!" They actually stopped and loaded up my wheelchair.

Christ, Hooper, good thing this was pre-9/11 because today Bunny would be shot by a sky marshal.

You know, Spokes, we've flown a ton of times since then. Hell, the rugby team must have been boarded this way over 40 times, plus many personal flights. Airlines really have gotten better at it over the years.

No, it's a dignity thief, Hooper. Why can't airlines offer a certain number of seats we can get in and out of without the dignity-sucking aisle chair? I don't know about you, but I don't like being treated like a duffle bag with a head.

Making commercial airplanes accessible doesn't require any major aircraft redesigns. It requires some serious thought about finding a better way—a little creativity that might involve removing one seat or better utilizing a part of first-class (right!). The reason it doesn't happen is that no one is squawking loud enough and long enough. And that's because there aren't enough wounded, aisle-chair warriors to say, "This sucks; we want dignified access." The airlines use the old "if it ain't broke, don't fix it" adage. You do see lots of people in wheelchairs at airports these days so you'd think there would be tons of complaints, but most of those folks can walk the short distance from the airplane's door to their seat and don't need aisle chair. Except for cases where wheelchair athletes and disability groups are traveling together, there aren't a lot of people who actually need aisle chairs from flight-to-flight, day in and day out. And, naturally, there will always be instances where aisle chairs are needed. But couldn't something be done to provide direct access to two seats (just two!), and, if there are no takers, give those seats to an able-bodied person? If non-walking wheelchair-users take those two seats first, then, like it is with wheelchair accessible parking, you're stuck looking for another place to park your ass, and you'll need to use the dignity-sucking aisle chair.

There's already a model. Quite by accident, Southwest Airlines has a couple of seats that a wheelchair-user can transfer directly into without the need of the dreaded aisle chair. When the rugby team flew Southwest, the high-pointers raced to get those seats. Gimps love them. It offers dignity and a level of independence.

I don't think the airline employees, who are generally very kind and helpful, like the aisle chairs either. Like us, they're stuck with them. It would be so much better all the way around, but like every accessibility issue it takes passion and enough committed people to take up the cause and fight the fight. Sorry to say, I will continue to swallow my pride and pretend it's no big deal.

You wimp, Hooper!

What, Ableman?! You want another major battle, because that's what this will be?

I want dignity, Captain Eddie.

Me too, maybe this is our next battle then.

Being in a hole can occur in many places—in a crowded room or sitting like Humpty Dumpty on an aisle chair. Dignity can be stripped away as quickly as the peel from a banana if we're not careful. It's 2015 and the problem hasn't changed, probably won't change either. Our dignity is left at the gate as we get loaded like freight via the same old aisle-chairs. The skies are friendly enough. It's the ground that gets downright nasty.

IV. Assholes and Handicapped Parking

This falls into the category of assholes never change. There have been cars keyed; tires flattened; notes written; insults hurled; police called; tickets written, and still the assholes insist on illegally parking in so-called "handicapped parking" spaces. Some people have it in their heads that it's ok to park there. The reasoning ranges from "they don't use it anyway" to "I'm only going to be a minute" to "I've got my mother's placard" to "screw them, I need a place to park" to just "fuck them." Whatever the reason, those parking-space pirates piss gimps off, but they absolutely infuriate friends and family members of the offended gimp. Grandmothers of family members with disabilities have been known to "key" an offender's car with the buckles on their purses. "Ooops," granny might say, "did I lose my balance and rub against that new Corvette or BMW?"

Spokes and I have had many such encounters with offenders, but we never damaged property. Egos maybe. Remember Spokes?

Oh, shit, do I. I was looking for parking at an Olive Garden and I saw this gimp-spot on my way in, but a woman pulled in just ahead of me and got the last accessible parking spot. I was ticked.

Why?

Well, I had to park like a block away, but she was there first so I figured, ah, tough luck. Anyway, I get out, and she must have been dilly-dallying around in her car doing something because when I went rolling by she had just gotten out of her car, and guess what?

What?

She wasn't freaking disabled. She had a long dress on and was walking perfectly fine.

That probably pissed you off even more.

Yaaaah! That was it. These asswipes get away with this over and over and over, and there's rarely a good shot at takin' 'em down, so I said to myself, "Not this time, Shirley."

Who's Shirley? Never mind. What did you do?

I rolled up to her and said, "Excuse me, mam, but don't assholes like you ever consider that another human being might need this parking?"

"Sir," she started to say, but I was having none of it.

"You just pull in here without any regard for anyone. Me? I can push so it's not that big of a deal."

"Sir," she again started.

"In a minute," I said. "But how about someone who can't go great distances safely. Do you ever think of them? Huh? Do ya? I hope you're proud of yourself."

Wow, Ableman, what a beat-down. What did she say?

Oh, nothing, she just lifted her dress to just over her knees exposing her polio braces all the way down to her shoes.

Holy crap!

Turns out she was nice about it, Hoop, even understood why I was pissed, but never again for me. From then on, I call the cops and hope they get there in time.

Remember, Spokes, assholes ruin other people's days so confrontation won't change them. And there are those with heart conditions, COPD, or like your Olive Garden friend who actually need the parking. Call a cop because a two hundred dollar fine will absolutely ruin a real asshole's day every time.

She did suggest that in the future that I simply ask if a person has a disability before I browbeat the bejesus out of them.

Why didn't we think of that?

Too busy being judge and jury, Fast Eddie.

So Spokes and I are against any type of instant justice, not because the law-breakers don't deserve it, but because you can't always be sure if they really are law-breakers, especially if they have a permit and leg braces you can't see.

Oh, Hoop, one more thing.

What's that?

Did we buy that woman you assaulted lunch?

That was you, Ableman, and, yes we did.

CHAPTER 14

THE POETRY OF FRIENDS

One thing I might say to someone who can't relate to poetry is: You don'thave to love all poetry. Do you love all music? Do you love every piece of art you see? Find just one poem you love, and speak it out loud. Your body, feelings, voice, and thoughts will come into harmony when you speak a poem that matters to you, and that can be incredibly healing.

Even people who supposedly don't like poetry have it all around them, but don't realize it, because they don't call it "poetry."

- Kim Rosen, Author of Written on The Bones

In many ways my friends themselves are poetry. Family and friends are what gets a newly injured person through the early dark patches of disability, and I have enough stories to fill ten books about how friends have helped me and loved me over the years. We all do, don't we? You don't need a disability to tap into that concept. Helping one another is human, poetic, and spiritual.

I've always been blessed with great friends—old friends and new friends. Some are in this book. Many are not because it's impossible to tell *every story*, to thank *everyone*. I know this isn't an awards show, but you each know who you are. You feel like poetry to me. I identify with some part of your essence, and I am so grateful for the rhythm and flow of your love and friendship.

195

I have been writing poetry since Vietnam in 1968. It was there that I met David Nye. It was he who encouraged me to write poems and songs and I've been doing it ever since. I call him Ho because when we were stationed in Vietnam together there was a little village nearby called Ho Nai (pronounced Ho Nye); I've called him Ho ever since. Ho kindled my creative side and I've cultivated that over the years into this go-to place, and that spirit is a large part of what gave me creative purpose and direction well beyond my first few years of disability. It will always be with me—the muse both comforts and pains.

Some thirty years later, Ho and I collaborated on writing about twenty songs. I wrote the lyrics and basic melody and Ho did all the music. We spent countless hours working on these tunes because we loved the work and because of the unconventional process we used: I could no longer play guitar after my injury, so I would record my version of a song a cappella and send it to Ho, and he would work his magic and put music to my effort and send that basic track back with changes and recommendations. I would then re-record using that track and send it back to him. Often Ho added his own guitar work, but mostly he uses Band In A Box (like GarageBand only better, according to Ho). BIAB provided a computer-generated choice of accompaniment: piano, bass, drums, strings, and horns—with adjustable tempo, adjustable key and choice of musical styles. After much back and forth, Ho added it all together and we had our songs. We called the CD *Shadow Figure*. It was a creative delight.

He told me at the time that he had set his own music aside for a good while, and that his studio and computer programs needed updating. Because he was helping me, it re-energized his love of his own music and he jumped back in to writing, playing, and performing. He now teaches ukulele. He plays in a band again (bass), and loves music the way he had before his passion got sidetracked. Whatever small part I played in that pales in comparison to what he did for me, because his poetry of action and passion are written into my heart.

There is poetry in every story if we look hard enough. I'm getting a little emotional, so I'm going to ask Spokes to tell the ramp van story, which has something resonating deep inside of it that makes me smile like a schoolboy.

Fair enough, Hooper, but I've got to change the names here to protect the innocent. My buddy, let's call him Don—Don Dawkins, The Dawk.

What the hell are you talking about? That's the guy's real name, Spokes. He's already in this book.

Oh, well, ok then, we won't change the names.

Dawk has a ramp van and he's way too proud of it. It's a van that has an electrically operated ramp that slides out and lets a wheelchair-user roll up into the vehicle.

Yeah, Spokes, we've all seen those or the ones with lifts.

Well, Hoop, Dawk has this drive-up steering in his van, so when he gets inside he just pulls his wheelchair right up to the steering wheel and drives from it.

How does he stay there?

He's got this little lock-down gizmo in the van and on the bottom of his wheelchair that snaps in automatically when he pulls up.

That sounds fast and easy, Spokes.

It is, very. He's in and on his way faster than an AB[22]. That's the problem.

Why, because it's not the way you get around?

No it isn't. I drive a car with a wheelchair topper, and it takes a little time for me to get in and out.

A little, Spokes?

Yeah, Hooper, a little, a few minutes. And Dawk takes great delight in reminding me of that fact as often as possible.

Really?

Yep, see we have lunch probably once or twice a month, and his standard operating procedure after lunch is that he rolls into his ramp van lickety-split, and, as he drives by me while I'm getting into my car, he shouts, "WHY DON'T YOU GET A RAMP VAN!"

To which you say?

I yell back my favorite action verb and its accompanying pronoun, and at the same time use the finger gesture that universally symbolizes that yell.

What does he do?

---

22 Able-bodied person

He smiles and drives happily away.

How long had that been going on?

Quite a while, until this one day...

Yeah?

Well, you have to visualize the scene: I'm in the parking lot—one of those strip-mall types. I'm just getting into my car and have my legs hanging out facing left. Just sitting and waiting for the Dawk to drive by and do his drill sergeant, ramp-van yell.

At the same time, walking in back of my car are a nice-looking, older couple who just got out of a mini-van of their own, one very much like Dawk's, and they were headed toward the strip mall cafe. Just then, the Dawk rides by in front of them and shouts—at me—in his loudest bellow ever, 'WHY DON'T YOU GET A RAMPVAN?!'

And what did you yell back?

Nothing. See, these folks didn't see me at all. As I said, they were behind my car. They just saw and they certainly heard what the Dawk barked out the window, and they thought he was yelling at them. So I just watched and listened.

And?

Well, they stopped. The woman looked at her husband and asked, "What did that loud man say we should get?"

"A ramp van, honey, I think he said we should get a ramp van," the confused man replied.

The woman looked back at her husband pensively and asked, "What's a ramp van?"

The man shook his head and said, "I don't know, but that loud fellow sure thought we oughta get one."

By now, Dawk had driven off, probably puzzled why I didn't tell him to go fuck himself.

Well, the couple continued walking out of earshot, but I could see the quizzical back and forth between them all the way into the restaurant—asking each other what just happened and what that boisterous man meant when he said, "Get a ramp van," and, of course, the ultimate question: what is a ramp van?

Now, this might only be funny to gimps, but to this day the Dawk and I think of this man and woman sitting having lunch, looking quizzically at one another while they're eating, and asking, what's a ramp van?

Thank God for Google, Spokes, or they may never have known.

Dawk and I laugh our asses off every time we talk about it.

Friends can also be family, like my two daughters have become such wonderful friends. My brother Don is a friend as well, a great friend, even though we don't usually think of each other that way. We're brothers and that itself is special, but we do get along quite well within most standards of friendship. In fact we often spontaneously call each other "pal," in the vein of the old *Honeymooners* TV show where Ralph and Norton called each other "pal" or "pal-o-mine." I think it's our way of saying we are both brothers and friends.

Don, like so many friends, was there for me after my injury in many ways that I took for granted. The list is long: He built my accessible house (We paid him but we got VIP treatment). He took me fishing down at the creek where the path up and down was hilly and bumpy, and he pushed me; he baited my hooks; and took the fish off when I caught one. He'd say that was easy work because I rarely caught any fish. I did get a ton of snags, though, and guess who got to free those up?

We watched Bear games together, usually at his house, and he literally pulled me up and down the stairs. We also played cards down in his basement, and he took me up and down both the house and the basement stairs. By the way, I positively hate being carried up and down stairs. Hate it! As soon as I leave the ground, it feels like I lose my dignity. But it never bothered me when Don did it because I trusted him and I wanted to be in that place with him to fish, watch football, play cards or whatever. My pride always surrenders to family and friends.

Introduced in Chapter Seven, my first accessible vehicle was the War Wagon. When a person with paralysis first learns how to drive with hand controls, it is a very confusing experience: One hasn't yet convinced the brain that one's legs no longer work, especially in reflexive situations like braking quickly. If a dog runs out in front of you, your brain is kicking like crazy to brake, but your leg isn't listening and you get discombobulated. That's why instructors in the passenger's seat have controls of their own. With practice, you quickly learn. But going out alone the first time is an adventure in anxiety, anticipation, and giddy independence. For me, it was marvelously frightening.

The Bears were playing the Packers, and I had made plans to go over to Don's house to watch the game. He only lived a few miles away. I was so careful with everything that I hardly recognized myself, planning every detail from getting into the van to transferring to testing all the controls and turn signals to making sure my seatbelt worked. Cindy helped. The van had a power seat that slid up and back about two feet or so using a short, sloped ramp-like base that operated on a mechanical worm rod. I got in the seat and used the power switch to lower me down and toward the steering wheel. All was well. I plotted my route (there was really only one way to get there) buckled up and drove over to Don's like I was handling nitroglycerin. For perhaps the first time ever, I obeyed every rule of the road ever written to the letter. I was flying high. I felt free!

I pulled up to Don's house excited beyond words. I made it! Nothing went wrong. I honked the horn and excitedly backed the seat up. The seat whirred all the way back and I began getting chills, bad chills, and then sweats. In gimp-land, chills and sweats are a warning sign that something is wrong— bladder, bowel, or pain of some kind. My first instinct was bowel problems. Damn, I thought! No game today. Then I looked down and saw that the seatbelt was still connected and it was squeezing the living shit out of me. I suddenly had a twenty-two inch waist! I was freaking out pushing on the release, but the buckle button wouldn't budge, so I scrambled to find the power control and slowly relieved the pressure. I sat there thinking, "Next stop, the ER."

Just then Don comes out and says, "Hi, pal." Then he noticed that I was as white as a sheet and asked, "What happened?"

I told him, and he helped get me into my wheelchair. He looked at my abdomen, and said it looked OK. I was panicked, though, because I was sure my insides had been crushed like a grape, and I asked, "Will you get in the drivers seat and hook up the seatbelt and run the seat back? You can feel and will know how bad it might be."

Don agreed and ran the seat back and said, "I gotta tell you, Bro, this thing is tight, but I don't think it caused you any damage." And he quickly lowered the seat and unbuckled the seat belt.

"Do it again," I said.

"What? Bro, I just did it."

"I know, pal, but you weren't there as long as I was."

"You know you could have told me that when I did this the first time," he said.

"I know, but I didn't think of it then. Come on, do it again."

So Don got back in the seat, buckled-up, and ran the seat all the way back. He sat for ten or fifteen seconds, looking a little uncomfortable, and then asked, "Is this long enough, pal?"

"Yeah, thanks, Bro. So you think I'm ok?"

"Yes, you're ok. Let's go, kick-off is in a few minutes."

We got out of the van, and he pulled me up the stairs, and in we went to watch the game. It wasn't all-good, the Bears lost to the Cheeseheads.

Yep, I love him. Not because of this story, but rather because of a lifetime of stories that I feel deep in my bones. Yes, of course, because he's my brother, but also because he is my friend.

This is a photo taken at a quad rugby tournament of my brother Don and I, and his sons Chad and Steve (standing). As with all my family and friends, we tend to laugh a lot.

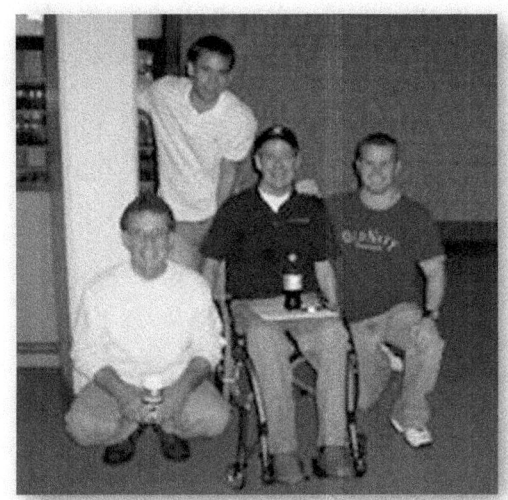

As Kim Rosen said, "poetry is all around us." As I age, I see more and more that friends are the verses of life that most warm or pain us—make us laugh and cry. We all have the poetry of our friends, because their actions heal and comfort us through the bad times, and they enjoy with us the good times. They even sometimes create bad things for us and we for them. We are affected greatly by those we love because we care, understand, forgive, and are forgiven.

Our verses may not make it to print like Rumi, Whitman, Cummings, Dickinson, Yeats, Dylan, or Mary Oliver. We enjoy, heal, and learn from those great writers, artists, and poets, but it's our friends and family who love us that write life's poems and songs onto our hearts. If we allow them, they paint our memories with their magic brushes of help, compassion and understanding. They sing to us in so many ways.

Birdsong
Birdsong brings relief
to my longing
I'm just as ecstatic as they are,

but with nothing to say!
Please universal soul, practice
some song or something through me!

Rumi

May we each sing a verse into our friends' life poems like they have into ours.

I don't think having a disability gives a special perspective into the power of friendship and love, but it certainly doesn't hurt. One of my favorite poems is e.e. cummings' "i carry your heart with me." It speaks to the universal power and scope of love in the cosmos. I cannot say it better. It ends:

and this is the wonder that's keeping the stars apart
i carry your heart with me(i carry it in my heart)

The last verse of a song I wrote best describes how I would like to be written into the hearts of those who loved me both with and without this onerous, yet precious gift of disability. Despite my flaws and tough road, I claim to be nothing more than a man who has lived and continues to live an extraordinarily happy life—a majority of which was happily lived from the seat of a wheelchair.

So when you think of me like yesterday
Celebrate that boy in the man
He was a song
That God jotted down
So sing it as best as you can